HOW THE FUTURE CAN SAVE US

How the Future Can Save Us

Fresh Perspectives on Waldorf Education

Principles, Methods, Curriculum

Stephen Keith Sagarin

SteinerBooks | 2022

SteinerBooks
An imprint of Anthroposophic Press, Inc.
PO Box 58, Hudson, NY 12534
www.steinerbooks.org

LIBRARY OF CONGRESS CONTROL NUMBER: 2022938973
ISBN: 978-1-62148-254-3

Printed in the United States of America

Contents

The Future

"Nor should we allow them to teach before they have gained an idea of how the past and the future affect our culture...and how that undefined rebel of the future can save us."

—RUDOLF STEINER,
Education as a Force for Social Change

INTRODUCTION

My title owes a debt to one of my favorite quotations from Rudolf Steiner's educational work. It refers to a paragraph from the last lecture of his *Education as a Force for Social Change*, given on August 17, 1919. Three days later, Steiner traveled to Stuttgart to conduct the training for the first teachers at what would become the first Waldorf school. But since there was no Waldorf school by that point, nor a "Waldorf education," Steiner may be seen addressing the education of teachers everywhere:

> We should not allow teachers to teach before they have gained a concept of the selfishness that strives toward the nearest god, that is, toward the angel. We should not allow teachers to teach before they have achieved an idea of the non-egotistical forces that determine human fate and exist spatially distributed over the Earth, that is, the nature of the archangels. *Nor should we allow them to teach before they have gained an idea of how the past and the future affect our culture...and how that undefined rebel of the future can save us.*

For Steiner, each of us is accompanied through life by an immaterial existence that tradition calls an angel. Our angels, according to Steiner, give us strength. And yet we may mistake our own angel, and its influence, for a larger god, and selfishly seek to inflict what is meant for us alone, what is true for us alone, on the rest of the world. "Angel," for Steiner, was a category far beyond the image of a winged, gown-clad being. An angel is a "set of powers," an immaterial mediator between our individual human lives and the spiritual, supersensible world that we also inhabit but of which we are largely unaware in our day-to-day existence.

For Steiner, human fate, larger than that of an individual, is associated with beings and powers he names the archangels. When we work with other human beings, we engage with the work of archangels.

Education prepares us for an unknown, uncertain future. Conformity, convention, and a lack of creative thinking and action will not serve us fully to face this future. We cannot know, and can only guess, what the future will bring, and we educate truly when we educate for inspiration—for insight and creativity—in the face of the unknown. We aim not to define our students, not to pigeonhole them according to our own inevitably partial and too-narrow view of the world they will inhabit and make. We aim to educate them while leaving them free to rebel, not for no reason, but for a reason, for a cause.

Who was Rudolf Steiner? We could say, in his call for a transformation of education in order to honor human creativity, that he was a "rebel with a cause." Who do we wish our students to become? In the best sense of the phrase, we hope they, too, will be rebels with a cause. And, in teaching them, we, too, may choose to become rebels with a cause.

☙

This book is about twenty years in the making. Following my dissertation, a history of Waldorf schools in the United States, I turned my attention to Rudolf Steiner's educational principles, methods, and curriculum. As with the history, I did not and do not see these as static, but, taking Steiner seriously, as living ideas with which we must continually engage, as we do with living beings, in order to understand, make sense of, and implement them for the healthful education of children.

Writing the history had awakened me to the various ways in which what we call "Waldorf education" came into being, slowly, over decades. Sometimes Waldorf education hews closely to what I understand were Steiner's intentions; other times, "Waldorf" practices seem actually to contradict what Steiner wished for education. Gradually making sense of what we do in Waldorf schools, piece by piece and point by point, led me to the creation of many of the essays in this collection.

At the same time, I was acutely aware that the needs and constitutions of students in the twenty-first century were different in significant ways from those of Germany in the 1920s. I am fortunate to be both a full-time high school teacher and administrator and a part-time teacher of teachers. These endeavors are mutually reinforcing. Teaching adolescents makes me a better teacher of teachers, and teaching teachers makes me a better teacher of teens. And, together, these jobs allow me to live with the tension between what Steiner said and did and what today's students require. Many of the essays in this collection examine this tension.

In 2008, I started a blog. Initially, I did this in order to share some of my ideas with my adult students and others in the United States, Europe, and elsewhere who were thinking about similar questions. Engaging students on my blog has been successful; engaging others, not so much. Regardless, as I worked through Steiner's education lectures—in order to teach them in faculty meetings, in study groups, with teacher education colleagues, and on my own—I wrote responses to what I found, and many of these found their way to the blog. Most of this book consists of what were initially blog posts, updated and rewritten as necessary.

My imagined audience for this book is primarily Waldorf school teachers and teacher education students who are working or will work to bring Steiner's education work to practical application in schools. I will also be happy if other teachers—those teaching in public and private schools that have no official connection with Waldorf education—appreciate this book. Independent of venue, my concern is almost exclusively with teaching and learning, not with schools. Although I have worked in private schools my whole career, I don't believe Steiner was particularly interested in founding lots of schools. His interest was in transforming education to make it practical and healthful for students in the industrialized world, particularly, in the aftermath of World War I, so that they could grow to make the world more peaceful and more just.

I can also imagine parents reading this book, particularly if they want to know more about Steiner's educational work, or if they are contemplating using "Waldorf education" in a homeschool. My hope is that they find an open-minded, thoughtful approach to Steiner's work that demonstrates the intensely creative but nonprescriptive mode in which he thought, spoke, and wrote.

And, finally, I can imagine former students—adults, high school, middle school, and those of any Waldorf school—reading this to learn more about what their education actually contained.

Readers who do not already have some familiarity with Waldorf schools and Steiner's work will still get a lot out of it—I hope—but may also scratch their heads at some points, as if to say, "What is all the fuss about?"

To this I would reply, "Exactly."

By inference, these readers will be able to tell that something is going on in Waldorf schools with which I take exception. To these readers, I say, take what you can and count your blessings if sometimes you don't really know what I'm talking about. For instance, if you've simply never heard of "math gnomes," your life is just fine.

My wish is that any who read this book find inspiration in their own ways to imagine an education for a future that's better than the present—more peaceful, more just, more humane—and to become rebels for this cause.

I also want to acknowledge that this book challenges conventional wisdom about several practices and components of what has become a somewhat standardized "Waldorf" curriculum, such as circle time, math gnomes, main lesson books, blackboard drawing, and Norse myths. And I believe it's important to be clear that by calling these into question, I am not asking anyone to stop teaching, in freedom and with insight, as they believe they ought best teach. I have worked in Waldorf schools for more than thirty years, and my wife and I sent both of our children through Waldorf schools. We have the deepest respect for anyone who devotes a life to teaching in a Waldorf school or tries to bring Steiner's ideas to students. But that does not mean that there's only one way to look at what we do in Waldorf schools, or that we cannot continually, conscientiously examine and alter and improve our practice.

GROWTH

1. PROTECTION AND LIBERATION

Picture a two-year-old with an iPad in her hands. Now contemplate these lines from Walt Whitman:

> There was a child went forth every day,
> And the first object he look'd upon, that object
>   he became;
> And that object became part of him for the day,
>   or a certain part of the day,
> Or for many years, or stretching cycles of years....
>
> The doubts of day-time and the doubts of night-time,
>   the curious whether and how,
> Whether that which appears so is so, or is it all
>   flashes and specks?
> Men and women crowding fast in the streets,
>   if they are not flashes and specks, what are they?
>
> ("There Was a Child Went Forth," *Leaves of Grass*)

Our children are pressured to grow up too quickly—they are sexualized without their consciousness or consent, or turned into tiny, desiring consumers, into naïve skeptics and ironists. From their first moments of consciousness, children are asked by advertisers to grow up faster, to buy, consume, and conform to the image we provide, to be sexy, hip, and cool. They are taught to be self-conscious, to be afraid to be themselves without our products.

And then, as soon as they get close to maturity, they are pressured not to grow up any further. They are told to stay young, impressionable, incomplete, malleable, insecure—to buy, consume, be sexy, be hip, and be cool. To continue to be adolescents. "Be a consumer," say the advertisers. "Be a pawn," say the demagogues. "Just don't think or perceive or act for yourself."

If we are not careful, our lives, and our children's lives, become the filling in an adolescent panini press.

Yet why are these mutually supportive pressures to grow up fast then to stagnate and stay forever young? It is because teens are in that in-between place, that nowhere land in which they have enough freedom, power, maturity, mobility, and intelligence to make choices, but not the developed judgment to always make wise or rational decisions. Recent research on teen brains shows this, although clearly advertisers have been aware of it for decades.

I don't mean to slander advertisers. Their efforts are successful because we allow them to be. We force them into ever more self-referential, ironic stances. But these work on us, too. No matter how savvy or critical you are, let me ask you: don't you believe, maybe secretly, that the products you use are the best? Maybe your progressive toothpaste won't make your teeth the whitest, but it will make them happy in a mouth of sea-salt and organic sage. And are your choices of cars or clothes the absolutely most rational? Or, like the rest of us, do you too often just have a rationale?

Also, who are these advertisers, these conniving merchants of images like Nike, McDonald's, Coca-Cola, Walmart, and GM? They are certainly not separate from you and me; they are you and me. They are local and worldwide employers, they drive globalization, they often transcend the rule of national governments. On average and by default, they represent us. And they are exquisitely sensitive to us and to our desires.

Even if you shun their products and buy locally and responsibly (though where did your jeans and your car come from?), you are complicit in and responsible for the world they have created. Sorry, there's nowhere else to go. Our world is a reflection of who we are collectively. What we truly don't tolerate doesn't last long.

And things will change.

This fear drives corporations and advertisers harder, and they in turn push you harder to get hooked on them earlier, to be less conscious of your affinity for their image.

Advertisers even have a technical term for your emotional attachment to their products: they call it "salience," and it's reflected in your blood pressure, your sweat glands, your respiration rate, even the dilation of your pupils. You can disdain Nike with your mind, but your body still wants those shoes. What you see isn't only what you get, it's also who you are.

I don't mean to slander young people, either. Adolescence is a wonderful thing. Teens are insightful and idealistic. They are innovative, eager, and open-minded. They promote change and are drawn to new ideas. They have little tolerance for the disingenuous. They have a powerful sense for what is fair and reasonable.

Also, please note: An image of adolescence is an image of the United States in the eyes of the world. As a nation we are hypocritical and dangerous, yes, and we are callow, naïve, and unconsciously selfish consumers. But we are also fair, idealistic, open-minded, and innovative. We are free-dom-loving, although we talk so often and so vehemently about freedom that it is clear that we have yet to achieve it. Maybe understanding ourselves as an adolescent culture helps to explain why it is so difficult for us actually to reach our own ideals.

In this context, our jobs as teachers and parents become clear. During childhood, we must protect children from influences that ask them to grow up too quickly. "Protection," we note, is one of the three primary principles of good elementary teaching that Rudolf Steiner offers in *Balance in Teaching*, his second, brief course for teachers in the first Waldorf school. (The other two are "reverence" and "enthusiasm.")

And then, when the pressure of the world shifts its weight, like a judo master, we move from guarding and protecting to liberating. We try to help our children and our students grow through adolescence to full, thoughtful, ethical, creative, inwardly-free maturity. Sadly, Steiner has less to say about this as an educational goal. The world in 1920 was clearly wide open to demagogues but less so to advertisers. Steiner's work as a whole, however, can be seen to aim at the development of true inner freedom.

Waldorf schools are fond of a quotation, lacking citation, that they attribute to Steiner: "Receive children in reverence, educate them in love, and send them forth in freedom." This quotation is a poor précis of a longer passage from Steiner's *The Spiritual Ground of Education* (p. 56):

> Who the teachers are is far more important than any technical ability they may have acquired intellectually. It is important that teachers not only love the children,

but also love the whole procedure they use. It is not enough for teachers to love the children; they must also love teaching, and love it with objectivity. This constitutes the spiritual foundation of spiritual, moral, and physical education. If we can acquire this love for teaching, we will be able to develop children up to the age of puberty so that, when that time arrives, we will be able to hand them over to the freedom and the use of their own intelligence.

If we have received children in religious reverence, and if we have educated them in love up to the time of puberty, then after this we will be able to leave their spirit free and interact with them as equals. Our aim is not to touch the spirit, but to let it awaken. When children reach puberty, we will best attain our goal of giving them over to freely use their intellectual and spiritual powers if we respect the spirit.

Clearly, Steiner's intention is not for us to throw our students out of the nest, as it were, to abdicate responsibility; this would be a mistaken notion of freedom. He is instead discussing freedom "of their own intelligence," of "intellectual and spiritual powers." The distinction between unqualified freedom and freedom of intellect is subtle, perhaps, but crucial. Without the assistance of teachers or parents or elders, adolescents left in freedom will flounder and flail. In the worst cases, they won't survive their own adolescence.

Between puberty and into adolescence, roughly between ages twelve and sixteen, there's a middle ground that Betty Staley calls a "vulnerability gap." This is a period of transition during which we as teachers and parents gradually, tactfully, appropriately, and consciously remove our protection; we liberate in order to encourage freedom and responsibility.

❧

2. Growth and Learning
in Three Easy Graphs!

Here's how your body grew. In your late teens or early twenties, you stopped growing in height. If you've put on a little weight since then, well, so have I.

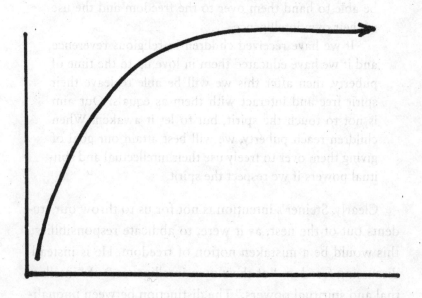

And here's how things that aren't alive often grow. Things like a pile of sand, built one shovelful after another, or the process of learning from a textbook, one paragraph or chapter after another.

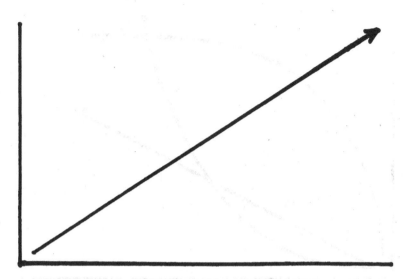

And here's how your intellect, which I might also call your mind or your spirit or your consciousness, grows. Unbounded by physical constraints, it is virtually unlimited. Or at least it is limited only by your interest and industry.

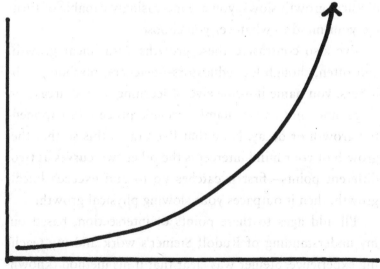

And here is what these three kinds of growth look like superimposed one on another.

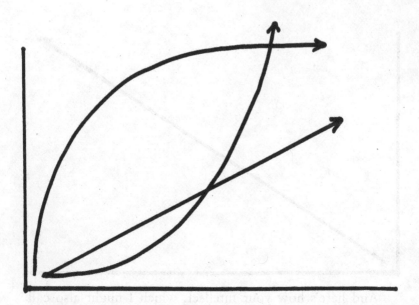

When you are very young, and most of your energy or life force is going into your physical growth, you don't have much energy available for intellectual growth. But, as your physical growth slows, you are increasingly capable of turning your mind to whatever you choose.

I've also contrasted these growths with linear growth. Too often, thoughtless educators—teachers, textbook publishers, you name it—conceive of learning as a staircase or slope, and not as a dynamic, organic process of exponential growth or decay. Note that I've drawn this so that the growth of your mind intercepts the other two curves at two different points—first it catches up to and exceeds linear growth, then it outpaces your slowing physical growth.

I'll add ages to these points of intersection, based on my understanding of Rudolf Steiner's work and my teaching experience. Steiner was clear that if his method (known in English since 1958 as "Waldorf education") were implemented, his students would initially appear to be "behind" those in more conventional schools that see education as sandpile-building. But, as they matured and their intellectual growth accelerated, they would catch and surpass those stuck with a shovel in a sandpile.[1] I believe fourth grade or age ten (or a bit later for some students) is the age at which we may often expect this to occur.

And, following a period of individuation in mid-adolescence, around age sixteen, as students find their own ways in the world, their intellectual development can accelerate in astounding ways.

METHOD

3. BACK-TO-BASICS ("MAIN LESSON")
TEACHING ACCORDING TO STEINER'S METHOD

Waldorf schools use block scheduling for many classes or courses, and school days almost always begin with a ninety-minute to two-hour "morning" lesson, sometimes erroneously called "main lesson," that contains much of the academic content of a school day. Much of what I've written below is most likely to be implemented in a morning lesson in a Waldorf school. But it's clear that this method—from conversation and discernment through new material, imaginative recapitulation, and reinforcement, to building anticipation—is applicable to all learning, to all classes, in a Waldorf school or virtually anywhere that anyone is teaching anything.

Let's say you have roughly two hours to teach a lesson. You have a lot to do.

Memory (Conversation leads to insight, discernment, and concept)

You begin with a conversation about yesterday's story or demonstration or happening. You call on your students' memories of yesterday's lesson. You ask them to talk about it, to form their own judgments, to practice discernment, and to develop concepts and even laws of nature. Some conversations will be open-ended; some you will guide to a conclusion. This daily conversation probably lasts anywhere from about five to thirty minutes, depending on the age of the students and your sense of the class. You do not ask students painfully or boringly or unnecessarily to "recall" or "retell" or "review" the lesson, but rather to re-inhabit it and extend it—with your assistance, to make it their own.[2]

Attention (Calls on the "whole being" of the student)

Then you present new concepts—letters, arithmetic operations, a comparison between two animals, a science demonstration, an event in history. In doing this you call for full attention—you call on the child's "whole being." So you do this as clearly and succinctly and efficiently as possible: possibly for five or ten minutes with younger children, and likely no more than twenty to thirty minutes even with seniors in high school.

Imagination (Generates interest and emotional investment—which leads to memory)

Next, you review what you have just presented. Students may create their own illustrations for letters (not always merely copying yours); they may work with piles of beans, for example, to study division. You work over what you have just told them, but in greater imaginative detail, fleshing out your description, calling on their imagination and feelings. What just happened in a physics demonstration? What did Caesar look like? What was his character? How had he come to stand on the banks of the Rubicon? And what does the Rubicon look like, anyway? Because you're now involving their imaginations, they won't tire so quickly, and you may devote more time to this part of the lesson, say thirty to forty-five minutes.[3]

In conversation with another teacher, I learned that the paragraph above may give the impression that I believe this part of a lesson should not be active or should be less active than it is in current practice. This portion of a lesson, in particular, however, calls for genuine, active learning and work and not just a teacher talking at the front of the room. Steiner intended lessons to be active—have students run the forms of letters, for instance! But this activity is different in two ways from a more general conception of movement as found, too often, in "circle time." The first is in the distinction between activity (running, writing, painting) that serves a conceptual purpose (learning the forms of letters, or the concept of a parabola) and activity in which consciousness is not on concept formation—activities such as eurythmy or singing; circle time activities, too often. And the second difference is in timing. Don't begin with a movement lesson; end with it, if you must.

Question (Builds anticipation and expectation)

Close each lesson with a statement about what students will learn tomorrow or a question to ponder, based on today's teaching, that they will discuss tomorrow.[4]

Story (Gives joy, interest, and basic knowledge)

End your main lesson with up to thirty minutes of a story that you tell—that you've learned (not necessarily memorized) or that you make up. Or, in older grades, it should be a story you read to the students.

Sleep (Consolidates learning)

Then, before addressing the topics of the lesson again, you allow students to sleep.[5]

Summary:

1. Conversation
2. Call on child's "whole being"
3. Review and expand in imagination (including activity)
4. Build anticipation
5. Tell or read a story
6. Sleep

⚜

4. TELLING TALES IN WALDORF SCHOOLS: A PERSPECTIVE ON RHYTHM AND REVIEW

Compare the two passages below. In the first, Steiner appears to speak against what many teachers in Waldorf schools practice—asking children to retell a story the following day. (Too often, they call this portion of a lesson "recall" or "review," although there's little in Steiner's work to justify these designations. More about what it should be below.) In the second, it appears he's speaking in favor of this practice of retelling a story.

But you must speak about it before you let the children retell the story. The very worst method is to tell a story and then to say: "Now, Edith Miller, you come out and retell it." There is no sense in this; it only has meaning if you talk about it first for a time, either cleverly or foolishly; (you need not always be clever in your classes; you can sometimes be quite foolish, and at first you will mostly be foolish). In this way the children make the thing their own, and then if you like you can get them to tell the story again, but this is of less importance for, *indeed, it is not so essential that the children should hold such a story in their memory*; in fact, for the age of which I am speaking, namely between the change of teeth and the ninth or tenth year, this hardly comes in question at all. (Steiner, *Kingdom of Childhood*, p. 64 [italics added])

Above all, we must try to cultivate as much simple speaking and conversation with the children as possible during the first year. We read aloud as little as possible, but instead prepare ourselves so well that we can bring to them in a narrative way whatever we want to tell them. Then we seek to reach the point where the children are able to retell what they have heard from us. We avoid using passages that do not stimulate the imagination and make as much use as possible of texts that activate the imagination strongly, namely, fairy tales—as many fairy tales as possible. Having practiced this telling and retelling with the children for a long time, we start in a small way to let them give brief accounts of experiences they themselves have had. We let the children relate something they like talking about. With all this telling and retelling of stories and personal experiences, we develop the transition from the local vernacular to educated speech by simply correcting mistakes the children make, without being pedantic about it. At first they will make many mistakes, but later fewer and fewer. Through telling and retelling, we develop in the children the transition from vernacular to educated speech. In this way, the children will have reached the desired goal by the end of their first year at school. (Steiner, *Practical Advice to Teachers*, pp. 168–169)

Here's what I derive from a comparison of these passages:

1. The primary point of telling and retelling is not the development of memory, but the development of correct speech. And that was more important for dialect-speaking Germans who needed to be educated in "Hochdeutsch" than it is for modern Americans. Not to say that our students don't need education in proper speech.

2. "As many fairy tales as possible" probably does not mean telling the same story over and over. How to judge pace: Are the students lively and interested, or are they fidgeting, yawning, and rolling their little eyes?

3. The first portion of a lesson, often somewhat erroneously called "review" or "recall," asks for the teacher to talk to the students, beginning in early grades by talking "cleverly or foolishly" about the story, and, in later grades, leading a discussion that involves contemplation, discernment, and coming to judgment, as in this passage:

> When the children arrive at school on the following morning they have, without knowing it, pictures of the previous day's experiments in their heads, as well as pictures of what—in as imaginative a way as possible—I repeated, recapitulated after the experiment. The children I then confront have photographs of the previous day's experiment in their heads. And I shall now reflect on yesterday's lesson in a contemplative way. Yesterday I experimented, and in reviewing the experiment I then appealed to the children's imagination. In today's lesson I add the contemplative element. In doing so, I not only meet the pictures in the

15

children's heads, but also help to bring the pictures into their consciousness.

Remember the progression: I teach a physics lesson, make an experiment, then recapitulate the stages of the experiment without the apparatus. On the following day, we discuss the previous experiment, contemplate it, reflect on it. The children are to learn the inherent laws. The cognitive element, thinking, is now employed. I do not force the children to have mere pictures in their heads, pictures they have brought with them from sleep, pictures without substance, without meaning. Just imagine the children coming to school with these pictures in their heads, of which they have no knowledge. If I were to immediately start with a new experiment, without first nourishing them with the cognitive, contemplative element, I would again occupy the whole of their being, and the effort they would have to make would stir up these pictures; I would create chaos in their heads. No, above all, what I must do first is consolidate what wishes to be there, provide nourishment. These sequences are important; they adapt to, are in tune with, the life processes.

...In the first part, I occupied their whole being; in the second, it is the rhythmic part of their being that must make an effort. I then dismiss them.

When they return on the following day they again have the spiritual photographs of the previous day's lesson in their heads. I connect today's lesson with them by a reflective, contemplative approach— for example, a discussion on whether Alcibiades or Mithradates was a decent or an immoral person. When I make an objective, characterizing approach on the first day, followed on the next day by reflection, by judgments, I shall allow the three parts of the three-fold human being to interact, to harmonize in the right way. (Steiner, *Education for Adolescents*, pp. 51–53)

(This book is now titled *Education for Adolescents*, but the lectures were a course given to the entire Waldorf school faculty and published as *The Supplementary Course* (supplementary to Steiner's first training course, which came in three volumes: *Foundations of Human Experience, Practical Advice to Teachers,* and *Discussions with Teachers*).

This passage draws our attention to other points worth considering:

1. The "review" occurs on the first day of a lesson, following a demonstration or presentation.
2. There is no mention of "circle time" or the activities included in it.
3. There is no mention of a three-day rhythm in Steiner's work on carrying a lesson overnight.
4. There is no mention of a "three-part" lesson in thinking, feeling, and will, as is too often claimed by teachers and teacher educators.
5. The progression Steiner outlines is this:

   a.) First day: Call on the child's whole being.
   b.) First day: Review—and add to the lesson— in imagination.
   c.) Let the child sleep.
   d.) Second day: Return to discuss, retell (after conversation), contemplate, come to judgment, discern, conclude.

∱

5. Teach to the Top, Aim for Epiphany

Here is part of a letter I wrote to my colleagues, some of whom are new to high school teaching, to our school, or both:

First, it's a principle at the school to "teach to the top" of each class. This is the easy part of our job—smart, motivated students practically teach themselves. We earn our money, so to speak, in helping those students keep up for whom our subject or the work of which we ask doesn't come easily. So please plan your classes and lessons for the "best" or "smartest" students in your class. Keep the pace high, and introduce topics—and write quizzes and tests—in a way that makes it possible for the weaker or slower students to pass, but really challenges the smartest or fastest students. Similarly, you can always give a range of assignments, from the direct and relatively easy to the complex and challenging. And, in any subject, you can always take the better students deeper, rather than asking them to work ahead or just giving them more work to do.

Not that we need Rudolf Steiner to tell us what to do, but his words on a related topic (in *Education for Adolescents*, p. 63) are worth considering: "First, the children must be interested in the subject. Genuine interest is connected with a delicate feeling of pleasure that must always be present.... We must endeavor never to bore the children."

Second, as we start the year, I believe it's really important to begin with a bang. Preview the year or your course, and introduce a topic that really grabs students' imaginations. (As an example, in precalculus, I used to discuss the principles and uses of parabolic reflectors and projectors and their focal points before we learned to calculate them. This is way more interesting than it sounds!) Students should go home with the sense that they're really going to learn something, that high school is different from elementary school, that this school is different from their old school. Ideally, each day for each student in each class should bring a moment of epiphany or revelation, an "Aha!" or "that's-so-cool" moment. Obviously, this is an ideal that we can't achieve, but it is one for which we can aim.

※

6. Good Teachers Don't Answer Their Own Questions

Once Harry Kretz asks a question, he stands and he waits. You can see that he is willing to wait while civilizations rise and fall, oceans dry up, stars die and fall from the sky, and the universe rumbles to an end, bang or whimper. He's present, attentive with his students, but waiting. He has asked a real question that a real student needs to answer for a real reason. He has not asked the question to prolong a class, to demonstrate knowledge, or to be pedantic, but because he's teaching young human beings and it's necessary for them to exercise themselves, to rouse their minds to activity, to make connections for themselves. Mr. Kretz asks a question that requires students to engage, to think, to draw new connections, to make an insightful leap across a previously uncrossed gap.

Mr. Kretz, one of the finest teachers I have known—patient, respectful, humorous—will tell you that many teachers, especially young, smart ones, don't really know how to ask questions. "Don't ask a question that you don't actually care if the students answer," he might say. And, once you've asked a question that you believe students should answer, don't do what too many of us do. Mistakenly, we wait a couple of seconds and then, impatient, the onrushing momentum of an untaught curriculum or the threat of silence or of boredom upon us, we answer it for ourselves. And our students relax back into watching the teacher's show.

"Er. Um." A student hazards a guess, voice rising at the end, questioning. Mr. Kretz absorbs this answer and asks another question.

Speaking of leaps, Helen Keller compared leaps of mind and dancing. Here's Merce Cunningham from Russell Freedman's biography of Martha Graham: "[I] felt [Helen Keller's] two hands around my waist, like bird wings, so soft. I began to do small jumps. Her fingers, still around my waist, moved slightly as though fluttering. I stopped, and was able to understand what she said to her companion: 'So light, like the mind.'" Sometimes, poetic truth and literal truth are the same thing.

✤

7. Stop Moving: "All Thoughts Previously Planted in the Head Simply Fly Away..."

Should a morning lesson begin with movement—you push the desks aside and, then—dancing, singing, eurythmy, bean bags?

Probably not. Sorry.[6] Here's Rudolf Steiner (in *Soul Economy*, p. 98): "By resuming ordinary lessons right after a movement lesson, we go against the child's nature."

Does your "morning circle" include a portion that might be called a "movement lesson"? Does it include "limb activities that stimulate the metabolism"?

If so, you may be interested to read this passage from Rudolf Steiner's *Soul Economy* (lecture 6, pp. 98–99):

If children have to sit still at their desks to do head work (more on this and classroom desks later), if their activities do not flow into their limbs and metabolism, we create an imbalance in them. We must balance this by letting the head relax—by allowing them to enjoy free movement later during gym lessons. If you are aware of the polar processes in the head and in the limbs and metabolism, you will appreciate the importance of providing the right changes in the schedule.

But if, after a boisterous gym lesson, we take our students back to the classroom to continue the lessons, what do we do then? You must realize that, while a person is engaged in limb activities that stimulate the metabolism, thoughts that were artificially planted in the head during previous years are no longer there. When children jump and run around and are active in the limbs and metabolism, all thoughts previously planted in the head simply fly away. But the forces that manifest only in children's dreams—the forces of suprasensory wisdom—now enter the head and claiming [*sic*] their place. If, after a movement lesson, we take the children back to the classroom to replace those forces with something else that must appear inferior to their subconscious minds, a mood of resentment will make itself felt in the class. During the previous lesson, sensory and, above all, suprasensory forces have been affecting the children. The students may not appear unwilling externally, but an inner resentment is certainly present. By resuming ordinary lessons right after a movement lesson, we go against the child's nature and, by doing so, we implant the potential seeds of illness in children. According to a physiologist, this is a fact that has been known for a long time. I have explained this from an anthroposophic perspective to show you how much it is up to teachers to nurture the health of children, provided they have gained the right knowledge of the human being. Naturally, if we approach this in the wrong way, we can, in fact, plant all sorts of illnesses in children, and we must always be fully aware of this.

I've heard for years, as a rationale for the movement portion of a morning circle: "Well, children used to walk to school and now they arrive flaccid from mom's minivan."

This may well be true. But a child walking, alone or with others, in an unstructured, ruminative or meditative or playful way, is not what morning circle embodies.

If you want to take your class for a brief, unstructured walk (in the fields or the woods, if available) before sitting at desks, that's something else.

Then, teach. Time is limited. You have a lot to do (maybe more than you've been doing, if you're going to be prepared to teach Milton's *Paradise Lost* once your students reach age ten).

And maybe end with movement, letting "the head relax— by allowing them to enjoy free movement later." That was my heady son's favorite class for years. It's called "recess." It didn't occur to him—and it wouldn't have mattered—that his teachers didn't actually think of it as a class.

And, to end this article, remember:

In singing, eurythmy, and physical education we spiri-
tualize the children. They are quite different beings at
the end of the lesson; there is much more spirit in them.
But this spirit wishes to consolidate, wishes to remain
with the children. We must not allow it to dissipate. We
can prevent it from dissipating quite simply and effectively by making the children sit or stand quietly at the
end of the lesson. We should try to maintain this calm
for a few minutes. The older the children, the more
important this will be. We should pay attention to these
things if we wish to prepare the children in the best
possible way for the following day. It is not in the children's interest for us to let them rush out of the room
immediately after a gym, singing, or eurythmy lesson.
We should, instead, let them calm down and sit quietly
for a few minutes. (Steiner, *Education for Adolescents*,
lecture 4, pp. 64–65)

☙

8. TAKING NOTES: A MIND-SPLITTING PRACTICE

Habit is a funny thing.

I went through school and college like everyone else,
writing down what teachers and professors had just said
while listening to what they were saying now. My hand-
brain lagged a few seconds behind my listening-brain. And
my looking-brain kept track of what was on the blackboard. Like everyone else, I could do this, and I did it,
decade after decade.

I noticed, however, by observing my students, not from
my own learning, that this wasn't necessarily a good way to
learn. As a teacher I realized how much time I spent waiting:

"Hold on, Mr. Sagarin, I'm not done copying from the board."
Or: "Yo, Mr. Sagarin, what did you just say?"
Or: "Can you say that again?"

I also observed the bizarre collection of misstatements and misunderstandings that crept into their work—less over time as I became more adept, but still...

So I've evolved a different approach. When I'm lecturing, I ask students to listen. Just listen. No note-taking. (Yes, they can doodle.) My students started calling this "Story Time with Steve." One even wrote a theme song about it.

The next day, I present a concise summary of the previous day's lecture. I write notes on the board, including proper spellings and dates and other necessary information. Students can copy without having to listen, without missing or mishearing. Sometimes, this process takes ten minutes or less. Sometimes it provokes a discussion that takes most of the period. In general, although I was worried that I'd lose time, I gain it. We cover more material more accurately. Student anxiety is less. Student attention is greater.

I don't use PowerPoint or email notes; I use students' memories to help me. Often, their phrasing is better—more concise, more accurate—than mine would have been. New angles and interpretations jump out of this review, insight that would have been lost if I'd simply rehashed yesterday's news.

What I've described is my ideal. Weekends, class time, project pressure, absence, and any number of other distractions keep the ideal at bay. Still, this way of working works for me, and I believe it's better for my students, for their comprehension, and for their retention.

I can't believe I didn't think of it years ago.

☙

9. NO APOLOGIES FOR A LIFE OF DOODLING

I doodle all the time—in meetings, on the phone, during student presentations in class. I have doodled for as long as I've been conscious, through elementary school, high school, college, and grad school. I have sets of things I like to draw—fountain pens, shoes, leafy vines—and hosts of "meaningless" geometric designs that appeal to me. I also draw things or persons in the room. I was always a good student, although I was taught to feel ashamed of my apparent inability to focus and prevent myself from doodling.

A few years ago, I decided to flout the accepted wisdom that it is wrong to doodle. I started to invite my students to doodle (and, if they liked, to knit or otherwise occupy their hands during class). I decided that it had not adversely affected my own learning and so it was unlikely to adversely affect theirs.

Instituting a "go-ahead-and-doodle" policy didn't solve all problems in my classes—students can get carried away, drawing comics with which they distract others. I also need to be more keenly aware of when (and during which activities in class) it's appropriate for students to doodle—when I am calling on them to remember what I am saying—and when it is better for them to be engaged in some other way. On the whole, however, I noticed that my classes were somewhat better behaved and I noticed that achievement didn't slip.

I didn't think of this as research, just as common sense, and I didn't bother to measure the effects of the change in my classes. Maybe I should have. Recent research, the five key points of which I have excised and highlight below, shows that doodling can assist memory recall. Finally, we doodlers can stop castigating ourselves for an activity that, in fact, may help us to sort out our memories and handle masses of detailed information.

So here are the five key points of the article, which is titled "Do Doodle: Doodling Can Help Memory Recall":

1. According to a study published today in the journal Applied Cognitive Psychology, subjects given a doodling task while listening to a dull phone message had a twenty-nine percent improved recall compared to their non-doodling counterparts.

2. Forty members of the research panel of the Medical Research Council's Cognition and Brain Sciences Unit in Cambridge were asked to listen to a two-and-a-half-minute tape giving several names of people and places, and were told to write down only the names of people going to a party.

3. The doodlers recalled on average 7.5 names of people and places compared to only 5.8 by the non-doodlers.

4. "If someone is doing a boring task, like listening to a dull telephone conversation, they may start to daydream," said study researcher Professor Jackie Andrade, PhD, of the School of Psychology, University of Plymouth. "A simple task, like doodling, may be sufficient to stop daydreaming without affecting performance on the main task."

5. Dr. Andrade concluded, "This study suggests that in everyday life doodling may be something we do because it helps to keep us on track with a boring task, rather than being an unnecessary distraction that we should try to resist doing."[7]

⇩

10. RHYTHM AND MEANING:
PLEASE DON'T EXTEND STEINER'S METHODS
FOR YOUNG CHILDREN INTO LATER GRADES

I recently taught a course for eighth graders at a nearby Waldorf school. As part of the class, as is common, we recited Rudolf Steiner's "Morning Verse."

I was taken aback by the rhythmic, singsong way the class recited, virtually devoid of meaning, like little children.

I talked to them about my preference, that older students need to think about what they say and imbue it with meaning, carrying the meaning over the natural pauses that line ends or rhymes introduce. We worked on it, and it felt so much better—a breath of fresh air.

And this week I read the following paragraphs in Steiner's *Soul Economy* (2003, pp. 138–139):

> Until the ninth year, children have a strong desire to experience inwardly everything they encounter as beat and rhythm. When children of this age hear music (and anyone who can observe the activity of a child's soul will perceive it), they transform outer sounds into their own inner rhythms. They vibrate with the music, reproducing within what they perceive from without. At this stage, to a certain extent, children have retained features characteristic of their previous stages. Until the change of teeth children are essentially, so to speak, one sense organ, unconsciously reproducing outer sensory impressions as most sense organs do. Children live, above all, by imitation, as already shown in previous meetings. Consider the human eye, leaving aside the mental images resulting from the eye's sensory perceptions, and you find that it reproduces outer stimuli by forming afterimages; the activity leading to mental

representation takes hold of these afterimages. Insofar as very young children inwardly reproduce all they perceive, especially the people around them, they are like one great, unconscious sense organ. But the images reproduced inwardly do not remain mere images, since they also act as forces, even physically forming and shaping them.

And now, when the second teeth appear, these afterimages enter only as far as the rhythmic system of movement. Some of the previous formative activity remains, but now it is accompanied by a new element. There is a definite difference in the way children respond to rhythm and beat before and after the change of teeth. Before this, through imitation, rhythm and beat directly affected the formation of bodily organs. After the change of teeth, this is transformed into an inner musical element.

On completion of the ninth year and up to the twelfth year, children develop an understanding of rhythm and beat and what belongs to melody as such. They no longer have the same urge to reproduce inwardly everything in this realm, but now they begin to perceive it as something outside. Whereas, earlier on, children experienced rhythm and beat unconsciously, they now develop a conscious perception and understanding of it. This continues until the twelfth year, not just with music, but everything coming to meet them from outside.

Toward the twelfth year, perhaps a little earlier, children develop the ability to lead the elements of rhythm and beat into the thinking realm, whereas they previously experienced this only in imagination.

These paragraphs and my experience support one of my broader contentions, which is that in general, Waldorf schools tend far too often to take Steiner's methods for younger children, age ten or younger, and extend them into later grades. Can we not do this? Thanks!

ψ

11. The Curious Case of the Missing Methods: On Chalkboard Drawing and "Main Lesson" Books

In 2019, in honor of the one hundredth anniversary of the founding of the first Waldorf school, I spent an exhausting three weeks helping to teach Rudolf Steiner's first, three-volume course for teachers. I could not help but notice that in this work—forty-six lectures in all—there is a curious absence of talk about two things central to our current practice of what we call "Waldorf education."

The first of these is blackboard drawings. Of them, there is not a word, other than a few references to suggest that children come to the board to draw or paint, say, making curved and straight lines or painting blue and yellow patches. (If they're drawing or painting at the chalkboard, we might wonder how can they be working in their "main lesson" books?)

The second is "main lesson" books. The only reference to notebooks of any kind in all these lectures is this (in *Practical Advice to Teachers*): "It would be very good if during these years [ages thirteen to sixteen] they were to keep a notebook in which to record the processes of soap manufacture, cigarette production, spinning, weaving, and so on."

At the same time, I read about the discovery of a series of blackboards that had been undisturbed since 1917 at a public school in Oklahoma City.[8] The blackboard images were lovely, and included beautifully handwritten text on a variety of subjects as well as rich, evocative drawings. And all of this was done in chalk of many different colors.

I also looked at old student notebooks from the 1920s and 1930s, which are commonly available for sale on eBay and Etsy. It is worth searching for them just to see their beauty, and the history they contain. They, too, show a variety of handwritten text and evocative drawings, also in ink of many colors.

From this I conclude that in the early twentieth century chalkboard drawing and student notebooks were common teaching techniques, ones that Waldorf schools have kept alive as the rest of the world has generally moved on.

Given Steiner's requests that we teach imaginatively and that we appeal to and develop students' aesthetic sense during elementary school, it's fair to say that current Waldorf school blackboard drawings and notebooks are often more beautiful than their earlier counterparts—handwriting aside. A lot of that old handwriting can only be described as amazing.

Meanwhile, this does not mean that blackboard drawings and notebooks are not good teaching tools or techniques. But it does mean that they arise from an older culture that is broader than "Waldorf education" alone. Therefore, we may hold these practices more lightly and look elsewhere for the essential value of our work. Some blocks may not need a book—for another course, other projects may suffice or be even better teaching tools. And the hours spent on blackboard drawings may sometimes be better spent preparing a lesson.

If you find value in blackboard drawing and having students complete notebooks, don't stop. But educate parents and colleagues not to be too critical if an otherwise loving, creative teacher chooses not to have students work so much in their books. Or, similarly, don't be too critical if another teacher gives less attention to blackboard drawing. Although these can be great teaching tools, they can be dogmatic practices that slow and even impede the creative transformation of education that Rudolf Steiner envisaged.

🌾

12. Moving through a School Day: Three Different Kinds of Physical Activity

Waldorf schools—and lots of other schools that don't chain kids to desks—promote learning through physical activity and movement, especially given how "movement starved" many children are. It's clear that there are (at least) three different kinds of educational movement, each of which serves its own purpose and each of which may occupy its own place in a school day.

It's also clear that separating things as clinically as I am about to do below isn't really possible in real life. There is lots of room for overlap and blurred lines. But I believe the distinctions below are helpful in thinking about how we teach and how children learn.

1. Free play

Taking a walk in the woods. Riding your bike to school. Playing pick-up soccer with your friends. Digging to the center of the Earth. Shooting hoops. Jumping from puddle to puddle. Catching frogs or crayfish.

Spending time with no teacher and no instruction.

Rudolf Steiner has little to say about free play, but it's clear that it is healthful for children and that we should create opportunities for it, especially in natural settings, particularly for children who are otherwise deprived of this. Free play can happen before school, during recess, or after school—or all three.

2. Conceptual activity

Movement that supports conceptual, cognitive development, e.g., using pebbles or other manipulatives to learn arithmetic operations. Drawing, painting, and modeling (in support of a lesson; otherwise, see skill building, below). Making geometric constructions. Doodling.

The teacher is teaching math or history or literature or geography, or almost any academic subject, and not focused on teaching a skill.

Rudolf Steiner is clear enough that this sort of activity belongs in morning lessons ("main lesson") at the appropriate time. Learning should often be active, even when teaching more contemplative subjects.

3. Skill building

The focus here is on movement that develops skill, such as singing, eurythmy, playing musical instruments, dancing, form drawing, gymnastics, physical education, knitting, calligraphy, javelin throwing.

The teacher is teaching the activity in which students are engaged.

Rudolf Steiner is really clear that this last category belongs *after* morning lessons, not in "circle time" before a lesson. If you include "circle time" or "morning circle" in your morning lessons (realizing that you cannot find words from Steiner on this topic), consider moving it to the end. It may not have occurred to Rudolf Steiner that we would confuse these categories and introduce skill lessons (such as recorder playing, singing, clapping games, and dancing) prior to morning lessons when, really, we should be encouraging free play. His words on the topic are clear enough:

If children have to sit still at their desks to do head work (more on this and classroom desks later), if their activities do not flow into their limbs and metabolism, we create an imbalance in them. We must balance this by letting the head relax—by allowing them to enjoy free movement later during gym lessons. If you are aware of the polar processes in the head and in the limbs and metabolism, you will appreciate the importance of providing the right changes in the schedule.

But if, after a boisterous gym lesson, we take our students back to the classroom to continue the lessons, what do we do then? You must realize that, while a person is engaged in limb activities that stimulate the metabolism, thoughts that were artificially planted in the head during previous years are no longer there. *When children jump and run around and are active in the limbs and metabolism, all thoughts previously planted in the head simply fly away.* But the forces that manifest only in children's dreams—the forces of suprasensory wisdom—now enter the head and claiming [sic] their place. *If, after a movement lesson, we take the children back to the classroom to replace those forces with something else that must appear inferior to their subconscious minds, a mood of resentment will make itself felt in the class.* During the previous [movement] lesson, sensory and, above all, suprasensory forces have been affecting the children. The students may not appear unwilling externally, but an inner resentment is certainly present. *By resuming ordinary lessons right after a movement lesson, we go against the child's nature and, by doing so, we implant the potential seeds of illness in children."* (*Soul Economy*, p. 98, italics added)

We try, as much as possible, to *teach the more intellectual subjects in the morning, and only when the headwork is done are they given movement lessons,* insofar as they have not let off steam already between morning lessons. However, after the movement lessons they are not taken back to the classroom to do more headwork. I have already said that this has a destructive effect on life, because while children are moving physically, suprasensory forces work through them subconsciously. And the head, having surrendered to physical movement, is no longer in a position to resume its work. It is therefore a mistake to think that, by sandwiching a gym lesson between other more intellectual lessons, we are providing a beneficial change. The homogeneous character of both morning and afternoon sessions has shown itself beneficial to the general development of the students. If we keep in mind the characteristic features of human nature, we will serve the human inclinations best. (ibid., p. 131, italics added)

CURRICULUM

13. FREE THE MATH GNOMES

During a panel discussion on the future of Waldorf education, the moderator asked me to identify a "myth" about Waldorf education. My go-to myth is math gnomes.

In the 1940s, Dorothy Harrer, then a teacher at the Rudolf Steiner School in New York City, needed an imaginative way to teach her students math. She couldn't turn to Europe, as most, if not all, of the continental European Waldorf schools were closed during the war. She couldn't turn to colleagues at other schools in the U.S., as there weren't really any. She couldn't easily turn to Steiner's works, as many of them hadn't yet been published, let alone imported or translated. And she couldn't turn to experts at a Waldorf teacher education program, as such programs didn't exist in the U.S.

There were probably resources from Rudolf Steiner and Hermann von Baravalle—Steiner's mathematician colleague, then in the U.S.—but who knows if she could get her hands on these, or if she was even aware of them.

Yet it was Mrs. Harrer, a humanities person and former public-school teacher, who dreamed up the math gnomes, wrote them down, and, eventually, published them in her book *Math Lessons for Elementary Grades*. I don't recommend it. But if you want to see what I'm talking about, this is the source.[9]

Her math gnomes, which have no basis in Steiner's work, and which actually contradict his recommendations for teaching math, have become the default position for many or most Waldorf elementary school teachers.

I asked Ernst Schuberth, a German Waldorf teacher and teacher educator with a doctorate in mathematics, if he had heard about them. He smiled and replied, "No, vat are zees mass gnomes?" They do not exist in Germany or, probably, in other countries. I do, however, recommend Schuberth's elementary math books, *Teaching Mathematics for First and Second Grades in Waldorf Schools* and *Mathematic Lessons for the Sixth Grade*.

After the panel discussion, a friend who is a former Waldorf school teacher and I chatted. He related how he had not used gnomes, but had invented, if my memory is correct, a prince, instead.

Then, a couple of days later, I received a sincere email from a former student, now teaching second grade, wrestling with how to bring some math concepts to her students. She knows my position on the gnomes, and was wondering about possibly using fairy-tale animals.

So here's the point that I'm trying to make: It's not about the gnomes, the princes, the animals, or characters of whatever size or shape or background!

Math brings the immaterial, the conceptual, the spiritual into the material world. Steiner recommends beginning with a pile of mulberries. Or beans. Or pieces of paper. These are real. Fairy-tale anything—gnomes, animals, princes, whatever—are not, at least not when it comes to teaching math. (If you don't believe in gnomes, then why on earth would you introduce them in math class? If you do believe in gnomes, why on earth would you trivialize them by asking them to teach arithmetic to young children?)

There are lots of sources, beginning with Steiner and von Baravalle, and continuing through Schuberth, that are intelligent, thoughtful, anthroposophical, true to math and true to the world into which we bring math, that do not personify what should really not be personified.

This is not to make anyone who used or uses gnomes, princes, or animals feel bad. We are all doing the best we can. I mean that sincerely. A former trustee with whom I worked, to avoid saying that something was bad or wrong, would jokingly say that it was "suboptimal." When we recognize that our performance is suboptimal, then we should change. We don't need to feel bad, we just need to do better. There's no shame in being wrong. We're all wrong much of the time.

There is shame, however, in rationalizing bad practices because of history or ideology. There is shame in not doing the research once a practice has been seriously called into question, in order to decide for yourself whether or not you will continue it. And there is shame in continuing stubbornly because it's easier than changing.

Free the math gnomes.

✤

14. Teaching Arithmetic Without Gnomes

If you are interested in teaching math without using gnomes, you may wish for guidance on what actually to do. So, for your ease of use, I have, throughout this chapter, compiled quotations on arithmetic and teaching math from about a dozen key Rudolf Steiner lecture series on education, including Steiner's initial course for teachers, his next two courses at the first Waldorf school (*Education for Adolescents* and *Balance in Teaching*), his two courses given in England (*A Modern Art of Education* and *The Kingdom of Childhood*), and a few others.[10] While these are not comprehensive, they certainly cover the territory, at least until teaching math through approximately third grade, because, in my experience, this is where the gnomes live and from where they need to be freed. Most of the quotations found here are also referenced, often in somewhat briefer form, in E.A.K. Stockmeyer's *Curriculum for Waldorf Schools*, a guide I heartily recommend.

So, let us begin with Steiner's basic point of view on teaching math.

1. Begin from the whole.
2. Introduce division first, then subtraction, then addition, and, finally, multiplication.
3. Use examples from real life. (This seems like a gnome-freeing injunction.)
4. Address these operations to students according to their temperaments.

And here is Steiner on the introduction of arithmetic:

Let's start with addition, and first see what our view of addition should be. Let's suppose I have some beans or a heap of elderberries. For our present task I will assume that the children can count, which indeed they must learn to do first. A child counts them and finds there are 27. "Yes," I say. "27—that is the sum." We proceed from the sum, not from the addenda. You can follow the psychological significance of this in my theory of knowledge. We must now divide the whole into the addenda, into parts or into little heaps. We will have one heap of, let's say, 12 elderberries, another heap of 7, still another of say 3, and one more, let's say 5; this will represent the whole number of our elderberries: 27 = 12 + 7 + 3 + 5.

We work out our arithmetical process from the sum total 27. I would allow this process to be done by several children with a pronounced phlegmatic temperament. You will gradually come to realize that this kind of addition is particularly suited to the phlegmatics. Then, since the process can be reversed, I would call on some choleric children, and gather the elderberries together again, this time arranging them so that 5 + 3 + 7 + 12 = 27. In this way the choleric children do the reverse process. But addition in itself is the arithmetical rule particularly suited to phlegmatic children.

Now I choose one of the melancholic children and say, "Here is a little pile of elderberries. Count them for me." The child discovers that there are, let's say, 8. Now, I say, "I don't want 8, I only want 3. How many elderberries must you take away to leave me only 3?" The child will discover that 5 must be removed. Subtraction in this form is the one of the four rules especially suited to melancholic children.

Then I call on a sanguine child to do the reverse process. I ask what has been taken away, and I have this child tell me that if I take 5 from 8, I'll have 3 left. Thus, the sanguine child does the reverse arithmetical process. I would only like to add that the melancholic children generally have a special connection with subtraction when done as I have described.

Now I take a child from the sanguine group. Again, I put down a pile of elderberries, but I must be sure the numbers fit. I must arrange it beforehand, otherwise we find ourselves involved in fractions. I have the child count out 56 elderberries. "Now look; here I have 8 elderberries, so now tell me how many times you find 8 elderberries contained in 56." So, you see that multiplication leads to a dividing up. The child finds that the answer is 7. Now I let the sum be done in *reverse* by a melancholic child and say, "This time I do not want to know how often 8 is contained in 56, but what number is contained 7 times in 56." I always allow the reverse process to be done by the opposite temperament.

Next I introduce the choleric to division, from the smaller number to the greater, by saying, "Look, here you have a little pile of 8; I want you to tell me what number contains 8 seven times." Now the child must find the answer: 56, in a pile of 56. Then I have the phlegmatic children work out the opposite process: ordinary division. The former is the way I use division for the choleric child, because the rule of arithmetic for the choleric children is mainly in this form of division.

By continuing in this way, I find it possible to use the four rules of arithmetic to arouse interest among the four temperaments. Adding is related to the phlegmatic temperament, subtracting to the melancholic, multiplying to the sanguine, and dividing—working back to the dividend—to the choleric. I ask you to consider this, following what N. has been telling us.

It is very important not to continue working in a singular way, doing nothing but addition for six months, then subtraction, and so on; but whenever possible, take all four arithmetical rules fairly quickly, one after another, and then *practice them all*—but at first only up to around the number 40. So, we shall not teach arithmetic as it is done in an ordinary curriculum. By practicing these four rules, however, they can be assimilated almost simultaneously. You will find that this saves a great deal of time, and in this way the children can work one rule in with another. Division is connected with subtraction, and multiplication is really only a repetition of addition, so you can even change things around and give subtraction, for example, to the choleric child. (*Discussions with Teachers*, pp. 48–50)

So Steiner asks us to base our teaching on "real life," "practical life"—not gnomes. To this end, here are some supporting quotations:

Your method must never be simply to occupy the children with examples you figure out for them, but you should give them *practical examples from real life*; you must let everything lead into practical life. In this way you can always demonstrate how what you begin with is fructified by what follows and vice versa. (Ibid., p. 156, italics added)

Suppose you had such an example as the following, taken from real life. A mother sent Mary to fetch some apples. Mary got twenty-five apples. The apple-woman wrote it down on a piece of paper. Mary comes home and brings only ten apples. The fact is before us, an actual fact of life, that Mary got twenty-five apples and only brought home ten. Mary is an honest little girl, and she really didn't eat a single apple on the way, and yet she only brought home ten. And now someone comes running in, an honest person, bringing all the apples that Mary dropped on the way. Now there arises the question: How many does this person bring? We see him coming from a distance, but we want to know beforehand how many he is going to bring. Mary has come home with ten apples, and she got twenty-five, for there it is on the paper written down by the apple-woman, and now we want to know how many this person ought to be bringing, for we do not yet know if he is honest or not. What Mary brought was ten apples, and she got twenty-five, so she lost fifteen apples.

Now, as you see, the sum is done. The usual method is that something is given and you have to take away something else, and something is left. But in real life—you may easily convince yourselves of this—it happens much more often that you know what you originally had and you know what is left over, and you have to find out what was lost. Starting with the minuend and the subtrahend and working out the remainder is a dead process. But if you start with the minuend and the remainder and have to find the subtrahend, you will be doing subtraction in a living way. This is how you may bring life into your teaching.

You will see this if you think of the story of Mary and her mother and the person who brought the subtrahend; you will see that Mary lost the subtrahend from the minuend and that has to be justified by knowing how many apples the person you see coming along will have to bring. Here, life, real life, comes into your subtraction. If you say, so much is left over, this only brings something dead into the child's soul. You must always be thinking of how you can bring life, not death, to the child in every detail of your teaching. (*The Kingdom of Childhood*, p. 79)

At first one should endeavor to keep entirely to the concrete in arithmetic, and above all avoid abstractions before the child comes to the turning point of the ninth and tenth years. Up to this time keep to the concrete as far as possible, by *connecting everything directly with life*. (Ibid., p. 126, italics added)

In this way, you can extend to all of arithmetic as an art the method of always going from the whole to its parts. (*Practical Advice to Teachers*, p. 9)

This said, I have heard people use the argument that they or a respected colleague have used math gnomes and found that their students liked them and learned math successfully. This is, unfortunately, no argument at all. Human beings learn math using all kinds of methods, even bad ones. Steiner is concerned that we begin from the whole so that we do not lead students into a materialistic (that is, acquisitive, parts-to-whole, atomistic, reductive) view of things. He is concerned that we use examples from real life to connect otherwise abstract math with its proper place in the world. We awaken genuine interest and enthusiasm (and awakening these requires artistic teaching) when we don't sensationalize our work by adding gnomes, but link our students' activity to what they know of the activities in the world and lead them to a conceptual understanding of mathematical truth and beauty.

ψ

15. WHAT WOULD STEINER SAY... ABOUT PAINTING WITH CHILDREN?

If Rudolf Steiner walked into a Waldorf school painting class today, what might he notice, and what might he say? (I don't wish to offend anyone who believes I'm being impertinent by putting words in Steiner's mouth, but my intention, through reference to what Steiner is recorded as having said, and also to what there's no record of him ever saying, is to make more immediate what would otherwise be dry.)

Q. What about all that wet-on-wet watercolor painting?

A. Believe it or not, I never said anything about that! I only said that the *paint* should be liquid. Yes, it's a way to keep the paper flat and to have the colors bump up against one another in a beautiful way, but it's not necessary, and it's certainly not something to carry on year after year through elementary school.

Q. What about paintings of one color only?

A. I never said anything about that either! Why limit the children's experience? Is this a meeting of German rectitude and American Puritanism? That's not what I intended! I spoke about individual colors, of course, but every reference that I made to children's painting exercises concerns at least two colors, that is, something that offers a comparison, a contrast that can give rise to a feeling in a child's soul. Don't confuse the theoretical with the practical! And don't confuse my esoteric lectures for adults with my recommendations for teaching children.

Q. What about restrictions on the colors that children are "allowed" to use? No black and no green? Primary colors only, but without true red or magenta or rose?

A. In lectures for adults, I included black, green, magenta, and white as "image colors," as opposed to the primary "luster colors," but I never said children should be limited in their experience of color. You certainly should not overuse black, and you may want to consider when you introduce it and the other image colors, but I never spoke of a restriction on color when working with children.

And while I did mention a teacher who was working with primaries only, this was just an example. I said, "In Dornach, Miss van Blommestein has begun to teach through colors, and they are making good progress. I have seen that it is having a very good influence. We allow the children to work only with the primary colors. We say, for instance, 'In the middle of your picture you have a yellow spot. Make it blue. Change the picture so that all of the other colors are changed accordingly.' When the children have to change oné color, and then change everything else in accordance with that, the result is a basic insight into color." Notice that I have the teacher ask the students to make the change. You all stand in front of the students and you do it for them. That's not helpful if you do it too often!

Also, don't forget that just before talking about Miss van Blommestein, I prefaced my remarks by saying, "In art, you can do different things in many different ways. It is not possible to say that one thing is definitely good and the other is definitely bad" (*Faculty Meetings*, pp. 297–298).

Q. *What about mixing the paint so thin that red is pink and other colors are washed out?*

A. I never said anything about that. Strong colors can be thinned out if you like, but weak colors will always be weak.

Q. *Cutting the corners off a sheet of paper?*

A. I never said anything about it.

Q. *Every teacher has to paint every year with every class in every grade?*

A. I said things that actually contradict this. I said, "It does no harm to interrupt the painting class for a few years and replace it with sculpting. The instruction in painting has a subconscious effect, and when the students return to the interrupted painting class, they do it in a more lively way and with greater skill. In all things that depend upon capability, it is always the case that if they are withheld, great progress is made soon afterward, particularly when they are interrupted." Then I said, "We cannot expect all the teachers to be well-versed in painting. There may be some teachers who are not especially interested in painting because they cannot do it, but a teacher must be able to teach it without painting. We cannot expect to fully develop every child in every art and science" (*Faculty Meetings with Teachers*, p. 716).

Q. *So, what did you say something about that you don't see in Waldorf schools today?*

A. I was very clear about an early lesson in painting. I said, "You need not hesitate quite early on to take out a box of paints and set a glass of water beside it (indeed, it is a good idea to conduct such lessons quite soon with the children). After you have pinned white paper to the blackboard with drawing tacks, you take up a brush, dip it in the water and then into the paint, and make a small yellow patch on the white surface. When you have finished, you let each child come to the blackboard and make a similar small patch. Each patch must be separate from the others so that in the end you have several yellow patches. Then you dip your brush into the blue paint and put blue next to your yellow patch. And you let the children come up and put on the blue in the same way. When about half of them have done this, you say: 'Now we shall do something else; I am going to dip my brush in the green paint and put green next to the other yellow patches.' Avoiding as well as you can making them jealous of one another, you let the remaining children put on the green in the same way. All this will take time, and the children will digest it well. It is indeed essential to proceed very slowly, taking only a very few small steps in the lesson. The time then comes for you to say: 'I am going to tell you something that you will not yet understand very well, but one day you will understand it quite well. What we did at the top, where we put blue next to the yellow, is more beautiful than what we did at the bottom, where we put green next to the yellow.' This will sink deeply into the children's souls. It will be necessary to return to this thought several times, but they will also puzzle away at it themselves. They will not be entirely indifferent to it but will learn to understand quite well from simple, naïve examples how to feel the difference between something beautiful and something less beautiful" (*Practical Advice to Teachers*, pp. 52–53).

Most teachers don't even try this! Of course, you must be authentic; you can't lie. If you yourself do not believe or find that blue and yellow are more beautiful than green and yellow, you could say, "You can clearly see that there is a stronger contrast between the blue and yellow than there is between the green and yellow." But not to do it at all?

I was also concerned that the students not become slovenly by painting in their books without stretching the paper first. I said, "I think painting instruction for the lower grades needs some improvement. Some of the teachers give too little effort toward technical proficiency. The students do not use the materials properly. Actually, you should not allow anyone to paint on pieces of paper that are always buckling. They should paint only on paper that is properly stretched. Also, they should go through the whole project from start to finish, so that one page is really completed. Most of the drawings are only a beginning" (*Faculty Meetings with Teachers*, pp. 715–716).

I also advocated the enlivening effect of painting on a tinted or colored background, but I hardly ever see teachers trying this. Why not? I said, "We should introduce children to color as early as possible, and it is helpful to let them use colored paints on both colored and white surfaces" (*Practical Advice to Teachers*, pp. 34–36).

You teachers. You often don't do what I recommended, and you rationalize and institutionalize all kinds of things that I never said anything about.

⇓

16. "Where Does Steiner Say We Have to Teach Stories of the (Catholic) Saints in Second Grade?"

A teacher educator once texted this question to a few colleagues, including me.

We didn't know. So we looked it up.

At the end of the first of Rudolf Steiner's *Discussions with Teachers*, he spoke briefly about and gave a list of stories for each grade, first through eighth. Here's the list:

Stories by Grade

1. A fund of fairy tales
2. Stories from the animal realm in fables
3. Bible stories as part of general history (Old Testament)
4. Scenes from ancient history
5. Scenes from medieval history
6. Scenes from modern history
7. Stories of the various races and tribes
8. Knowledge of the races

Interestingly, there is no mention of the saints. "Fables," meanwhile, include Aesop's, of course, but also others—Abenaki, African, Indian. It would be hard to think of a traditional culture that didn't have its own fables regarding the animal world.

Also, in one of the "curriculum" lectures appended to *Discussions*, Steiner adds this:

> At the beginning of the second grade, we will continue with the telling and retelling of stories and try to develop this further. Then the children can be brought gradually to the point of writing down the stories we tell them. After they have had some practice in writing down what they hear, we can also have them write short descriptions of what we've told them about the animals, plants, meadows, and woods in the surroundings. (*Discussions with Teachers*, pp. 185–186)

So, for saint stories we have to turn to other sources. Caroline von Heydebrand's *Curriculum of the First Waldorf School* uses the term *legends* to describe further second grade stories. Certainly, stories of the saints are legends, but there are many other legends—from Sufis and Jews to others from all over the world. A large number of stories that may be included as "legends," that teach in a way similar to fables, are parables, and Steiner (without specifying second grade) speaks frequently of them. He even goes so far in *Faculty Meetings* to say, "We need to write a good Jesus legend."

But just to be crystal clear, I find nothing wrong with the beautiful stories of many, many saints! I'm glad both my children heard them. But when a school or teacher is too rigid regarding a curriculum—and a world—that allows for and demands greater inclusivity and breadth, it's just shortsighted to hew to something that Steiner didn't actually say!

Some schools, in moving away from a too-Christian curriculum, have included historical figures, "good people," such as Gandhi, Mother Teresa, and Martin Luther King, Jr. These figures are not legendary, however; they're historical. It is a disservice to them and to our students to present them as legends. All too soon, students will learn of their many human failings, and may become disillusioned.

Our job is not to insist on an ahistorical hagiography of actual historical figures; it is to tell stories that are poetically and metaphorically true and include "morals" as fables do (though Steiner is clear that, in his view, we should not make these morals explicit to young students). These are stories that include much to ponder, that connect young students to their world in a good and meaningful way, and that teach on several levels.

Similarly, although less common, this curriculum doesn't include legends in a contemporary sense—tall tales, ghost stories, or "The Legend of Sleepy Hollow." They are modern stories modeled on the ancient tales we're to tell.

A clue to this view is in the list that began this article. Generally speaking, the list begins with ancient stories, with the least concrete or literal truth in them, and moves through time into actual history. This is explicitly true in Grades 4 through 8, in which stories leave ancient myth and move toward modern history.

Looking at this list raises another point. The story content for Grades 4 through 8, particularly, anticipates academic content by a full year. Thus, the teacher can tell stories of Rome in fifth grade and then teach the history of Rome in sixth grade. The tremendous boon to students is obvious: when the teacher begins to teach sixth grade history, his or her students can recall all they know from the previous year, and feel the structure that forms and adds to what they already know. How beautiful!

A related point is this: Steiner *does not say* that the stories we tell are to become content for our academic classes and our main lesson book illustrations! To this end, allow me to share a quotation by E.A.K. Stockmeyer, another teacher at the first Waldorf school:

> It has never been clarified how Steiner wanted the story material fitted into the main lesson. It appears to me that he wanted the teachers to set aside a special time during the lessons [at the end of what we call "main lesson"] when educational and artistic treasures should be offered to the children without the compulsion to learn, purely because of the inherent educational value, so that the children should learn to know the world in a way which they could enjoy. (Stockmeyer, *Rudolf Steiner's Curriculum for Waldorf Schools*, p. 29)

What joy!

⚜

17. Do You Have to Teach Norse Myths in Waldorf Schools?

Rudolf Steiner must have said that Waldorf schools should teach Norse myths in fourth grade, right? Every Waldorf school does it, and it's hard to come up with something more typical of what many include when they use the term *Waldorf education*.

Not so fast.

Here's a note I received some time back from Adam Jacobs, a student at Rudolf Steiner College in Sacramento:

I've been doing some research on Steiner, and nowhere can I find an indication where he recommends teaching Norse mythology in fourth grade. Clearly Steiner does have a reverent attitude toward it, above and beyond other cultures' mythologies (see *The Mission of Folk-Souls*, lecture 9), but I'm not sure he recommends it in fourth grade. Is this another Waldorf myth? Help!

Here's my reply:

It's certainly true that the first series of stories that Steiner recommends (at the end of *Discussions with Teachers*, 1) does not include Norse myths, but refers instead to "stories from the ancient world" and "stories from the Middle Ages." And I can't find it *anywhere* in any of Steiner's first dozen series of lectures on education! So, I guess it is a "myth" in the sense that it's crept into the curriculum as (ostensibly) "given" by Steiner when, in fact, it appears not to be.

And here's part of his reply to my reply:

The arguments over whether or not we can replace Norse mythology are *ad nauseam* and, in my opinion, put up roadblocks for Waldorf education expanding in an international context. If people knew that his only indication was ancient stories, that would change the picture. [Some] Waldorf teachers...would prefer to use Norse myths themselves, for whatever reason. [But,] because they are actually deeply uncertain about the validity of that claim, they feel the need to hang it on the coatrack of Steiner. Through Steiner, as a divine authority, they claim the merciless authority to believe that they are deeply, irrevocably *right*.

52

And here's my final reply to the reply to the reply:

> The more I look, as with so many myths, the less I find.
> I believe that 'ancient stories' for Germans were, often
> and largely, Norse myths. But Steiner himself appears
> never to have prescribed them (it's harder to find what
> someone didn't say than what he did say!). This leaves
> us, as teachers of adults and of children, a lot more
> freedom—and less reason for dogma of any kind—to
> choose what to teach. Waldorf education, I find, is far
> more a method than a content, anyway.

So, there you have it. Ancient stories, including but not
limited to Norse myths. Thanks, Adam. Enjoy, everyone!

ψ

18. AFTER THE "NINE-YEAR CHANGE": SHOULDN'T YOU READ *PARADISE LOST* WITH TEN-YEAR-OLDS?

Dear Colleagues,
Does this passage reflect your teaching practice?

> As teachers, whenever we approach growing human
> beings, we must note the striking contrast between the
> pre-puberty and post-puberty years. Let us take a con-
> crete example: There is Milton's *Paradise Lost*, which
> would be good to use in our lessons. The question is,
> when? Those of you who have thought through what
> has been said so far and have understood my remarks
> about the right time to introduce narrative and descrip-
> tive elements will find that *this work by Milton (or
> epic poetry in general) would be suitable material
> after the tenth year. Also, Homer will be appreciated
> best when taught between the tenth and the fourteenth
> years.* On the other hand, it would be premature to use

Shakespeare as study material at this stage, since, in order to be ready for dramatic poetry, students must at least have entered puberty. To absorb the dramatic element at an earlier age, students would have to drive something out of themselves prematurely, which, later on, they would definitely miss. (*Soul Economy*, p. 229, italics added)

For almost all of us, I suspect, the answer is "no," so we are due for some reflection. Clearly, Steiner is not asking us to teach the whole texts of Milton or Homer, nor, however, is he asking us to teach simplified "children's" versions of these texts.

Further, this passage may call into question the common introduction of Shakespeare into elementary school curricula. How many schools traditionally perform a Shakespeare play, usually a comedy or romance, in seventh or eighth grade?

Steiner is asking us to take relevant passages, prepare the students to learn from them, and then, finally, to read and discuss them.

For instance:

Hence, you should always try to leave the actual reading of a piece until last, first dealing with everything you can give the children to help them understand it. If you prepare for the reading as well as you can ahead of time, then you will not work like a pedant, but help make the whole piece clear and understandable, and thus enhance the children's enjoyment and satisfaction." (*Discussions with Teachers*, pp. 70–71)

Steiner asks us to prepare similarly for the recitation of poetry—and Milton and Homer (and Shakespeare, of course, at the right age) should be both read and recited:

54

The lessons in a school should be arranged in a way that allows recitation to be closely connected to the musical element. The music teacher should be in close contact with the teacher of recitation so that instruction in one subject follows directly on instruction in the other and so that a living relationship between the two is established. It would be particularly useful if the music and recitation teachers could work together in the classroom, so that each could point out the links between the two subjects. This would be one way to eliminate a truly dreadful teaching method that is still very much prevalent in our schools—the abstract explanation of poems. This abstract explanation of poetry, verging almost on grammatical dissection, spells the death of everything that ought to work on the child. Interpretation of poems is quite appalling.

You will protest that interpretation is necessary if the children are to understand the poem. I would counter that all the lessons must be structured to form a totality. This has to be discussed in the weekly meetings of the teachers. If a poem is to be recited, then the other lessons must encompass whatever might be necessary to shed light on the poem. The teachers must properly prepare the children to bring to the recitation lesson whatever they need to help them understand the poem. If, for instance, the children are to recite Schiller's "Der Spaziergang," the cultural, historical, and psychological aspects of the poem can quite easily be presented to the children, not by going through the poem line by line but simply by telling them whatever they need to know about the content. The recitation lesson itself must focus on the artistic presentation. (*Practical Advice to Teachers*, p. 43)

Toward the end of this period of child development, ages ten to fourteen, Steiner refers several times to reading Schiller:

> *A teacher:* How far should I go in history before turning to something else? In the seventh grade, I have gotten as far as the end of the Caesars in Roman history, and in the eighth grade, I am at the Punic Wars.
>
> *Dr. Steiner:* Make an effort to get to Christianity and then do two months of German. Do Goethe and Schiller in the eighth grade.
>
> [*Dr. Steiner tells an anecdote about a child who is asked, "Who are Goethe and Schiller?" The child replies, "Oh, those are the two statues sitting on the piano at home."*]
>
> You should teach German history differently in the eighth grade than in the seventh. (*Faculty Meetings with Teachers*, p. 63, Jan. 1, 1920)

We should consider the English equivalents of Goethe and Schiller, if any, for our English classes. And, in history teaching:

> *A teacher reports about the humanities in the seventh and eighth grades. There is a discussion about Goethe's biography and also his* Poetry and Truth, *as well as Schiller's* Aesthetic Letters.
>
> *Dr. Steiner:* I would recommend Herder's *Ideen zur Philosophie der Geschichte der Menschheit* [Thoughts on the Philosophy of Human History], in which he presents the human being as a summation of all the other natural realms. World History should continue right up until the present. (Ibid., p. 66, March 8, 1920)

I would recommend that you have the eighth grade read the first chapter of Schiller's *Thirty Years War*. They can learn a lot from that. It contains many things that go up to the present. (Ibid., p. 239, Mar. 23, 1921)

I think that Schiller's historical works would be good reading. Such books are excellent for thirteen- and fourteen-year-olds. (Ibid., p. 339, Apr. 28, 1922)

So we're talking about Grades 4 through 8, and the names Steiner recommends—Milton, Homer, and Schiller—are among the greatest, most profound writers and thinkers of the literary world. It's worth pointing out that Milton is English, Homer is Greek, and only Schiller is German. Clearly, for Steiner, their ideas and the expression of these ideas are generally more important than the language or culture that these authors represent. (A good English stand-in for Schiller—poet and philosopher—would be Samuel Taylor Coleridge, a founder, with Wordsworth, of the Romantic movement in England.)

I don't think asking us to reevaluate our teaching based on these indications represents a turn toward more "academic" teaching, though it could certainly have that effect in the wrong hands. Steiner is not asking us to make our teaching harder or to load on challenging work that's over the heads of our students—or that asks them to grow up too fast. He's letting us know that he believes children from about the age of ten on can begin to contend with the deepest and most beautiful ideas that human literature and history (and, eventually, philosophy) have produced. What are these studies, the humanities, called in German? *Geisteswissenschaften.* The spiritual sciences.

It's also worth pointing out that elsewhere in his work Steiner takes Milton to task for perpetuating a dualistic or twofold view of the world, a world that finds its way even into the movie "Animal House"—an angel on one shoulder and a devil on the other, whispering in our ears. Steiner's view was that Milton mistook Lucifer for a "good" angel, calling on our egotism, rather than our individual moral imagination, to conform our behavior to "goodness." So, when I learn that Steiner recommends reading Milton with, say, fifth graders, I imagine teaching in such a way that I can help my students, in lively conversation in the days following our reading, to see that this dualistic representation is shallow or false. It strikes me, too, that *Paradise Lost* is an excellent two-word description of the change that children go through between roughly ages nine and ten.

҂

19. SOME FACTS ARE JUST BELIEFS IN SHEEP'S CLOTHING: ON TEACHING AND HUMAN CAPACITIES

We educate children, and children are human beings.

But what is a human being?

An image of a human being underlies all attempts at education, tacitly or explicitly. Sometimes this image is a metaphor—a garden to be tended, a computer to be programmed. Sometimes it's an expression of our beliefs—humans are born in original sin and so must have this beaten out of them. These images reflect beliefs about what it means to be human.

And beliefs, no matter how fervently we may believe them, are dangerous. Belief, in the modern world, almost instantly becomes ideology—hardened, defended, asserted. As Sarah Vowell writes in *The Wordy Shipmates*, "The only thing more dangerous than an idea is a belief.

And by dangerous I don't mean thought-provoking. I mean: people might get killed."

Yet what about beliefs in anthroposophy?

As Owen Barfield wrote in *Romanticism Comes of Age*, "What is anthroposophy? Believing (some would answer), without a shred of evidence, everything that Steiner chose to say. And that is exactly what it is not.... I cannot think it is unduly paradoxical to say that it is really a kind of betrayal of the founder of anthroposophy to believe what he said. He poured out his assertions because he trusted his hearers *not* to believe."

So let's put aside belief. Maybe instead we could look at these things called "facts." Sadly, it turns out that facts aren't as factual as we might hope. Or believe.

Samuel Arbesman, a medical doctor, studies what he calls the "half-life of facts." In his book by that very name, Arbesman carefully examined old medical papers on treating liver disease. He discovered that it took about forty-five years for us to completely discard half of what we had accepted as fact, what we believed to be true, in treating liver disease. The half-life of a medical fact about liver disease is forty-five years.

He went on to study many other kinds of facts. His conclusion is that at any moment only about half the facts that we accept to be true are actually true or, to be more precise, will still be held as true roughly half a century from now.

Some facts, like facts about mathematics, are durable, almost eternal. And some facts, like facts about celebrities, may be falsified tomorrow.

In general, however, about half of what we think we know is wrong. And we don't know which half. Doctors used to prescribe cigarettes to promote healthy lungs. Europeans used to hold that women's uteruses wandered around within their bodies, prompting strange behavior; this is the concept of the root of hysteria.

What we are dealing with here is this: Some facts are just beliefs in sheep's clothing.

So if our image of teaching a growing human being is not to be based in fact, and is not to be based in belief, in what, then, can it be based?

My answer is this: in growing human capacities. Human capacities include such qualities as patience, courage, fairness, generosity, and kindness.

Let's take patience as an example.

Imagine yourself a teacher, sitting at your desk in a nearly empty classroom, waiting patiently for Timmy to finish his lunch so that you can dismiss him and head to the teacher's room for a cup of herbal tea.

First, you must be conscious of your patience. Simply enduring, unconsciously, as the hamster in the back of the classroom seems to be doing, is not really patience.

Second, you must be in a relationship, however taxing, with someone or something in the world. In this case that someone is Timmy.

Third, you must be inwardly active. Patience must be continually renewed or it fails. And when it fails, when you scream at Timmy through a clenched jaw to finish the heck up and get out of the room, all your patience evaporates. You are not patient; rather, you are someone who tried to be patient and failed.

Fourth, capacities like patience make ethical demands of us. Is my patience a virtue? If I'm waiting for a temper tantrum to subside, it may be. If I'm waiting patiently to destroy my enemies, it may not be.

Fifth, and last, patience is a balance between the incessant demands of the world beyond Timmy and your selfish desire for that cup of tea. You know this sort of balance as a polarity, one only an active, imaginative human being can resolve.

At a professional development workshop during the first years of my life as a teacher, we young teachers were asked to imagine our retirement, and to write down how we wanted to be remembered by our students at the end of our careers.

We shared these with each other. I was the only Waldorf school teacher there, but none—not one—of the other teachers' responses had to do with course material or test scores or achievement. None represented beliefs or the teaching of facts. And for what did we wish to be remembered? A long list of qualities, including fairness, kindness, and generosity.

And I ask you, as a reader, to test this yourself.

Remember a favorite teacher. My guess is that she was good at teaching—that may be considered a given. She knew her subject and imparted it with enthusiasm and skill, engendering competence and a love of the subject in you. But I would also guess that what you remember most fondly are not her methods, her technique, her beliefs, or the facts she imparted, but some capacity or quality that she showed you. You remember her as the fairest, the most generous, the most caring.

So how do we teach capacities?

Not with worksheets. Not by impatiently demanding patience from our students. We do this only by working to strengthen those capacities within ourselves. And, in order to strengthen patience, let's say, we must examine and know ourselves from a higher perch than patience.

To that end, what are human beings? Human beings are beings who are capable of being better tomorrow than they are today, of continually increasing their capacities for things like generosity, fairness, courage, open-mindedness, and patience. According to Rudolf Steiner, when we give up this current life and slip into the next, we discard our beliefs and our knowledge. These do not avail us. Yet upon what do we build our future lives? We build them on the capacities we have developed here and now.

Can we say that each of these capacities is related to the others? Can we say that patience is a form of generosity, and also a form of kindness? Can we say that each is like a different color of a higher virtue, of love itself?

⚜

20. Rudolf Steiner's Only Known Reference to a Nature Table

When he was seven, Goethe built himself an altar to nature. He took his father's music stand and placed on it plants from his father's herbarium and minerals and crowned it all with a little incense candle that he lit by focusing the beams of the morning sun with a magnifying glass. This was an offering to the great god of nature—a rebellion against everything imposed on him by education. In the very essence of his nature, Goethe was always a human being longing to be educated in the way people ought to be educated today. (*Practical Advice to Teachers*, p. 104)

Clearly, this reference does not mean to suggest that this is what teachers "should" do, simply that *kleiner* Johann did this in rebellion against whatever he experienced of German education in the mid-1700s.

Do Germans or Austrians other than Waldorf teachers build nature tables, following Goethe?

Is there any other source for the nature table?

Inquiring elves want to know.

TERMS

21. WHAT DOES RUDOLF STEINER MEAN BY "SOUL"?

Rather than assuming that we know what Rudolf Steiner means by the term *soul*, and then agreeing or disagreeing with our own notions, I hope it's valuable to examine what he actually means. I believe this can help us get past terminology and on to realities.

1. By "soul," Steiner discusses our life of "sympathies" and "antipathies," the things we are drawn to and the things we are repelled by or seek to distance ourselves from.[11]

It is clear from conversations with students, however, that our colloquial interpretations of *sympathy* and *antipathy* need some clarification. Sympathy is not "good," and antipathy is not "bad." Both are necessary; it is good that we are repulsed by the odor of rotting food, for instance. More deeply, it's clear that we can only know in a conscious sense because of what Steiner calls antipathy—a distancing of knowing subject from known object. On the other hand, total sympathy, unification with everything, precludes consciousness and suggests paradise before the apple is eaten.

These considerations show how antipathy is linked with our capacity for thinking, a mental distancing or beholding. And sympathy—a movement toward—is linked with our capacity for action, our will.

Between these two forces or activities or capacities, mediating or dynamically balancing the tension between them, according to Steiner,[12] are our emotions or feelings. Every thought that is put into action carries with it at least a bit of emotion, if only the interest to see the intention carried out; every action that finds a mirror in cognition is also accompanied by emotion.

Our emotional lives, then, arise through the polar interactions of thinking and will. And, as a whole, these three capacities—to think, to feel, and to act—are what Steiner calls "soul."

2. By *soul,* Steiner also means that which, in us, unites our physical existence with our spiritual existence.

I write physical and spiritual "existence" deliberately. Those who translate and write about Steiner's work often refer to these forms of existence as "bodies," but I find this problematic and misleading. In English, the word *body* is too materialized and too objectified to be a proper translation from the German *Wesen,* which means "body," but only in the sense of essence or nature. *Wesen* is the noun form of the verb *wesen,* which means "to exist" or "to be present," so I believe *existence* captures the meaning well.[13]

The soul, then, is like the contents of a sandwich in which body and spirit are the bottom and top slices of bread.

To be more precise, Steiner often divides the soul into a lower soul, which he calls the "etheric existence," and a higher soul, which he calls the "astral." The lower soul, more plant-like, is that which animates the physical body, which, without the animations, would otherwise remain a lifeless corpse. The higher soul, more animal-like, is that through which we are sentient beings.

Understanding soul in these ways helps us to avoid jargon, which is necessarily divisive, and goes some way toward conceptual clarity. If we can agree, for instance, as parents and teachers, that we would like our children and students to think deeply, clearly, and insightfully, that we would like their emotional lives to be full and authentic, and that we would like their actions to be purposeful and ethical, then it hardly matters whether or not we use the word *soul* in discussing our work with them.

Meanwhile, I want to make clear that there are greater depths and intricacies to Steiner's conceptions of soul, but these build and expand upon the concepts I've shared here.

❧

22. What Does Rudolf Steiner Mean by "Etheric Body"?

In *Theosophy*, Steiner uses *Ätherleib* or *Lebensleib* to describe what is often translated as the "etheric body." We could also translate it as "etheric life" or even "life-life," which is obviously confusing. "Etheric existence" may be too vague, but "etheric body" is too constrained. So, perhaps we can find our meaning somewhere in between.

But let's get to the heart of the matter. In *Education for Adolescents*, Steiner spends parts of two lectures (6 and 7) describing ancient Greek perceptions of the etheric in the physical, based on their understanding of "four elements" (fire, air, earth, water) and how they manifest in the world:

> When the Greeks spoke of earth, air, fire, and water, they did not look at them as we do today. If you had asked one of those people who lived within the Greek

world conception—and there were still a good number of them in the fifteenth century, the later ones having read about it in books; our modern people sometimes take a look at it without understanding it—if you had asked one of them: "What is your idea of fire, of warmth?" the Greek would have answered: "I think of fire as being warm and dry." "What about air?" "I see air as warm and damp." The Greek did not think of the physical properties in fire and air but rather formed an idea. This idea contained the sub-ideas: warm and dry, warm and damp. The Greeks did not limit themselves to the physical appearance but imagined the elements as inner qualities. One had to raise oneself to something that could not be seen by physical eyes, that had to be grasped by thinking, in order to get to a knowledge of the elements, of what one then called the elements.

What did they achieve by this? They arrived at an understanding that corresponded to the etheric in the human being—the etheric body in its effectiveness. This understanding of the elements as inner qualities allowed them to experience the etheric body. Their experience was not that of being in the etheric body but rather in how the etheric body worked in the physical. (*Education for Adolescents*, pp. 101–102)

By contrast we can point to the views held especially by the ancient Greeks...views that are today dismissed as childish, as I said yesterday. But these views, correctly understood, provided the people with something else: the way they regarded the four elements—earth, air, fire, and water. As I pointed out, they did not regard the four elements as pictures of coarse sense impressions, coarse physical matter; they regarded them qualitatively. Fire contained at the same time the qualities warm and dry;

they thought of water as cold and damp. These living concepts that they connected to the elements could then be applied in several ways.

They applied them in the way they thought about their connection to earth, air, fire, and water—in which they saw pictures, quite definite pictures. They could apply them to the way, in the human being, that the etheric body activates the mixing and de-mixing, synthesis and analysis of matter. They could understand how the etheric body is working in the physical between birth and death. (Ibid., pp. 108–109)

I had read these words for years without understanding them well. Then, one serendipitous summer day, part of their meaning became clear to me.

In a clay sculpture class, we often begin by taking a hunk of clay and forming it into a smooth sphere. After a few minutes, I ask students to pass what they're working on to the person on their left (or right). We can continue working on the clay—smoothing the imperfections we inherit from our neighbor—or continue passing the clay, receiving in turn the work of each student in the room. And we notice immediately that each piece of clay is warmer or cooler or wetter or drier than our own. Some people communicate their warmth to the clay. Some dry the clay merely by working it. Each person's clay is different with regard to these qualities. So, in Steiner's terms, we experience the etheric existence of our neighbor in holding the clay we have just received.

We experience this immediately, directly, and comparatively. We don't experience it, at least at first, analytically. The clay is not "warm" or "cold"; it's "warmer than what I just held" or "cooler." To that end, we can have the same experience in shaking each other's hands. Your hand will be slightly warmer or cooler than mine, or slightly drier or damper.

On the same day, I participated in a brief observation of a plant, which turned out to be the large, colorful, daisy-like *echinacea*, growing west of the building in which our class met. In researching it later (I'm not a botanist or herbalist), I learned that *echinacea* is drought-resistant and prefers hot, dry conditions.

Based on earlier work with clay and this insight about a daisy, more clicked into place in my mind. Again, for decades, I'd heard (and repeated) that what Steiner means by "etheric" refers to the qualities that living organisms share with plants—that is, life—and not with minerals (which are non-living) or with animals (that is, sentience). This is true, as far as it goes, but a deeper understanding recognizes that plants express the conditions of their life by preferring conditions that are warm and dry, warm and wet, cool and dry, or cool and wet. Further, of course, they participate in the "mixing and de-mixing, synthesis and analysis of matter," preferring soil that has a particular mineral profile or acidity. They don't just "live," they express, in their living, the etheric conditions of their existence.

ψ

23. What Does Rudolf Steiner Mean by "Spirit"?

The word *spirit* is troublesome for many thoughtful Americans, and, regardless, its colloquial use is vague. What does it mean to have "school spirit," or to be in "good spirits," or to describe, well, just about anything as "spiritual"?

Rudolf Steiner's work, however, is based on a clear understanding of the concept of spirit. Without knowing what he means by it, it's hard to come to terms with his work at all.

1. The German *Geist* translates into English as "spirit," but these two words have subtly different meanings. *Geist* may often equally well be translated as "mind." So the German word *Geisteswissenschaft*, "spiritual science," can be translated as "science of the mind," as compared with *Naturwissenschaft*, "natural science." (Interestingly, the word *Geist* was imported or absorbed into English as "ghost," which is not what Steiner meant at all.)

2. When Steiner talks about "spirit" in his seminal education lectures, *Foundations of Human Experience* (formerly, *Study of Man*), he discusses spirit as manifesting in states of consciousness—wakefulness, dreaminess, or sleep. In this sense, spirit is consciousness, and consciousness may be acute (awake, alert), vague (dreamy), or absent (asleep).

Consciousness, in Steiner's *Philosophy of Freedom* and elsewhere, is the phenomenon that appears as the dynamic balance—often rhythmic—between thinking, on the one hand, and observation or perception, on the other. In thinking of something, we are awake to it. And, we may say, when we give ourselves fully to observation, we "sleep into" the phenomenon that we perceive.

Of what are we conscious? We are conscious of those things that we can conceptualize and perceive. This seems clear enough at first blush, but these categories are not fixed. As we grow older, our thinking may become clearer and sharper (to a point, if we're fortunate) and, sadly, our perceptual abilities are likely to fade—although our discernment within this narrowing scope may thrive (as in the case of Beethoven).

If I am blind, I simply cannot perceive what others see unless I am able to have surgery that allows me to see. (Yet even then, as Oliver Sacks describes and William James intuited, I will have to educate my consciousness around my new perceptions in order actually to "see.")

So, to stretch this a bit, let's say that angels are real, if immaterial, and that I cannot perceive them. I am angel-blind. No known surgery addresses angel-blindness, but, through the earnest application of contemplative exercises and self-development, according to Steiner and others, I may develop the capacities that allow angel-vision. My consciousness will expand to include angels, which I will then be capable of perceiving and conceptualizing.

3. Spirit is, according to Steiner and many, many others, that within us that is eternal. Soul is less so, and our physical body is almost entirely temporal. In this sense, our consciousness, in some form, exists prior to our birth and survives the death of our body.

To the extent that we find meaning in these concepts of spirit as teachers and parents, we may address our children healthfully. Do we wish our students' minds to perceive and think clearly, accurately, and without bias? Do we wish their consciousness to be awake to beauty, truth, and goodness? Do we wish for them to be mentally mobile enough to form clear concepts based on accurate, unbiased observation? Can we address these capacities through the education that we create for them? If we can answer these questions in the affirmative, then we are, at least on an introductory level, addressing them as spiritual beings, in Steiner's terms.

Further, if we conceptualize them as conscious beings worthy of dignity and care from earliest existence through old age and the gate of death, we also address them as spiritual beings.

And, if our concepts of spirit begin with clarity, they may grow, so that, even if we remain angel-blind, our consciousness of spirit, in Steiner's sense, enlarges beyond our current capacity to know or to imagine it.

🔥

24. What is Anthroposophy?

Before trying to say what anthroposophy is, I'd like to cut away some misconceptions or misunderstandings and say what it is not.

First, the word *anthroposophy* should not be capitalized in English. Germans capitalize nouns. English speakers capitalize only proper nouns, and anthroposophy is not one.

Second, you may know that Rudolf Steiner did not make up or invent the word *anthroposophy*. Cornelius Agrippa may have used it in the early 1500s. Thomas Vaughan, a Welsh philosopher, non-practicing physician, and Rosicrucian appears to be the first in print, in 1650. He was followed by Immanuel Hermann Fichte, one of the founders of German idealist philosophy; Friedrich Wilhelm Joseph Schelling, philosopher; Ignaz Paul Vitalis Troxler, a Swiss physician, philosopher, politician, and a student of Hegel; and Robert Zimmerman, a Czech-Austrian philosopher, who published a book called *Anthroposophie* in 1882. These German uses span a good hundred years prior to Steiner's activity.

Steiner was aware of and credited Zimmermann and also Fichte, Schelling, and Troxler, I believe. I don't believe he made mention of Agrippa or of Vaughan, who wrote under the pen-name Eugenius Philalethes, which means "Good Spirit, Lover of Truth."[14]

I point out Steiner's adoption of a word and, to a limited extent, its use by others because I find that adherents and opponents of Steiner both often seek to emphasize his uniqueness. Adherents do this to demonstrate how truly special he was, and opponents find his ideas easier to attack if he is isolated. Steiner's work is unique in some ways, but he is also part of deep intellectual and esoteric traditions, and should be seen in this context.

Third, anthroposophy is not belief in what Steiner said and it is not a body of knowledge. As a thought experiment, imagine that every "fact" in Steiner's work, such as karma and reincarnation, and blood and nerves, turned out to be false. Anthroposophy, as an attempt to recognize and value human existence in the world, will still be a necessary concern for human beings. Meanwhile, I don't believe that Steiner was actually wrong about everything, though I also don't believe he was infallible.

Fourth, anthroposophy is not an academic discipline, and should not stand in a university course catalog along with other disciplines or subjects like philosophy, anthropology, molecular biology, astrophysics, or art history. I hope we never have to see any university offer a degree in anthroposophy. As I hope to show, this would represent a complete misunderstanding of anthroposophy.

Fifth, anthroposophy is not a path of meditation, or meditation alone, or meditation tacked on to regular science or to conventional interpretation in the humanities. A scientist who performs her work as usual, within its conventional paradigm, often a reductive and mechanistic one, and who then, because of reading Steiner goes home, sits in her armchair, and meditates about her work in order to gain greater insight may, in fact, gain some insight, but will not necessarily be working anthroposophically. She may be valiantly trying to add a bit of the inner world to her work in the outer world, and she may actually have success in doing this. But this is merely using meditation as an instrument.

I once had a colleague who wished to write a paper on a topic in education. But rather than conduct due diligence and actually research his topic, he believed he could sit in his armchair and anthroposophically meditate his way to the insights necessary to write the paper. Needless to say, the paper was not very good.

Similarly, I have seen Waldorf school teachers sit in a circle and attempt to solve a problem in the school by meditating their way to a solution, without, again, conducting the investigations and having the conversations that might lay the groundwork for fruitful insight.

Further—and this is a bit of a tangent, but a relevant one—anthroposophy is not a religion.

Yet the issue of religion and Waldorf education is not a simple one, and I consider it comprised of three points of view. The first might be summarized by the idea that all education, all meaningful human endeavor, has, in the broadest sense, a religious component. As A. N. Whitehead wrote in *The Aims of Education and Other Essays*, "The essence of education is that it be religious." From this perspective, to speak of value, explicitly or implicitly, is to give evidence of a religious engagement with the world. This view is too broad to consider here, however, and does not necessarily distinguish Waldorf education from other methods.

The second point of view is that Waldorf education is religious in a more conventional sense because some ideologues, through misunderstanding and misapplication of Steiner's work, make it so. As Dorothy St. Charles, former principal of the Milwaukee Urban Waldorf School said in a 1994 radio interview, Waldorf education is not a religion, "but some people make it one."

The third point of view, and the more carefully considered, is that Waldorf education and anthroposophy, the method that underlies it, are not religions at all. In 2004, Douglas Sloan, former coordinator of the joint program in Religion and Education between Union Theological Seminary and Teachers College, Columbia University, New York, made this point eloquently as an expert witness in a lawsuit arguing that charter Waldorf schools, as religious schools, violate the First Amendment of the U.S. Constitution. He argued against this view as follows:

> By all scholarly criteria of what constitutes religion, anthroposophy is not a religion.... The attempt to define religion has been notoriously difficult, and the approaches to doing so are many. In general, there have been three main approaches.
>
> The first can perhaps be called the essentialist approach. Essentialist definitions tend to focus on the inner essence or substance, the metaphysical reality claims, of religions, and the relationships to these demanded of human beings by the claimed realities. One of the conceptual difficulties with this focus is that philosophers and others can make metaphysical and ethical arguments about the nature of reality without

advancing these as themselves constituting a religion, although they may well have implications for religion.

The second main approach to the study and definition of religion can be called the functional approach, and is probably the theoretical approach most favored by social scientists, although as I shall point out, some theologians also favor it. Functional definitions of religion stress the effects, the functions of religion, in actual life—the ways in which religion functions to fulfill basic human needs, both individually and communally. Different scholars stress different functions as the defining characteristic of religion. Among these various functional definitions are, for example, the cognitive—religion provides meaning systems for understanding and coping with life; the psychological—religion functions to meet psychological needs, such as a sense of security in the face of life's uncertainties, a sense of identity, a sense of purpose, and so forth; the social—religion serves primarily to provide values for social cohesion and the preservation of the social group; and the ideological (Marxist definitions of religion are a good example)—religion serves the power interests of governing elites by deluding the masses. Each of these taken by itself is decidedly reductionist, and, in order to avoid inordinate reductionism, most scholars attempt to fashion combinations of various functional approaches.

One form of functionalism, often utilized by students of religion, is that of the twentieth-century American theologian, Paul Tillich. Religion Tillich defined as expressing "the ultimate concern" of an individual or of an entire culture. Every person and every society, he argued, has its "ultimate concern" (often, to be sure, directed toward less than ultimate objective realities).

In fact, for Tillich, every culture is grounded in its own ultimate concern, to which it gives concrete expression. Culture itself as a whole is, therefore, the religious expression and activity par excellence.

"Religion," Tillich famously wrote, "is the substance of culture, culture is the form of religion." Tillich's position can be a good illustration of how the strength of the functionalist can also be its main weakness. The strength is that it enables one to see the religious functions, as noted above, of many human activities not usually recognized as religious: the state, the university, science, technology, the stock exchange, Sunday afternoon football, and so on. Each has its ultimate concern, and often its own "priesthood," paths of initiation, dogmas, sacred texts, and other marks of religion.

The weakness is that a definition which begins to apply to everything often ends up telling us little about anything.

In view of these various approaches, it is not surprising that one leading historian of American religion (Catherine Albanese, UC Santa Barbara), whose works I reviewed in forming my opinion, has observed that scholars have become increasingly less certain about what should be counted as religion as a general phenomenon. "In the end," she writes, "religion is a feature that encompasses all of human life, and therefore it is difficult if not impossible to define it."

In this light it is probably also not surprising that historians of religion turn mainly to the third approach to the definition of religion, namely, the formal. Scholars in the history of religion and comparative religion deal primarily with the actual religious forms manifested by concrete religious groups and movements. These religious forms include such things as beliefs and doctrines (creeds), ritual activities, forms of worship, sacred texts, and recognized sources of authority. The advantage and strength of this approach is that it is concrete and makes it possible to determine whether a group actually functions, not just religiously in general, a la Paul Tillich, for instance, but as a formal, identifiable religion as such. It also is possible then to distinguish it in detail from other religions and their forms, and to trace the actual development of a specific religion over time. In this perspective, a religious group is one that manifests and is organized around these common religious forms, albeit with its own distinct versions of them. This approach can also incorporate aspects of the first two approaches.

It is especially from the perspective of this third approach to the definition of religion, the formal, that I can meaningfully and concretely testify that anthroposophy is not a religion....

Anthroposophy is the name given by Rudolf Steiner to designate the way of knowing, the method of inquiry, that he established....

It is a wholly personal choice not only whether one follows Steiner's method of knowing and tries to develop it, but also whether, out of conviction, one accepts–or does not–Steiner's own results and content flowing from that method as he practiced it. If the principle of individual freedom based on knowledge is violated in following Steiner's indications, then the entire method is vitiated.

So now let us move into what anthroposophy is.

First, we may say that anthroposophy aims at a conscious reunification of the "inner" world of thinking and the "outer" world that we perceive, however imperfectly, through our senses. But the terms *inner* and *outer* are misleading. We perceive much of our inner life—emotions, for instance, or the values we hold—as somehow external to our innermost self but still within us, not in the world of cows and trees and grass. They are the changeable "me" that my less changeable "I" can perceive within me at any moment. And we know that our sense impressions, which arrive via undifferentiated nerve impulses, are somehow synthesized into a more or less coherent world within us.

Second, Steiner uses the phrase "spiritual science" and the term *anthroposophy* interchangeably. Yet, to be clear, Steiner was not attached to these names. In *The Child's Changing Consciousness*, he wrote:

> If I had my way, I would give anthroposophy a new name every day to prevent people from hanging on to its literal meaning, from translating it from the Greek, so they can form judgments accordingly. It is immaterial what name we attach to what is being done here. The only thing that matters is that everything we do here is focused on life's realities and that we never lose sight of them. We must never be tempted to implement sectarian ideas. (pp. 21–22)

Perhaps, accordingly, a good name for a true anthroposophist might be "Good Spirit, Lover of Truth."

Third, to use Owen Barfield's phrase, anthroposophy is "Romanticism come of age." Briefly, historians are apt to dismiss the Romantic era, of roughly 1800 to 1850, as a beautiful but ultimately impractical artistic response to the social, political, and economic upheavals of the Industrial Revolution in Europe and North America. Barfield believes this interpretation to be incorrect and argues that it misunderstands the possibilities of Romanticism, such as true individuality, regard for nature, and investigation of imagination as a human capacity. For Barfield, anthroposophy represents a more mature, more practical extension of

Romanticism—into fields like agriculture, medicine, education, and social policy.

One founder of the Romantic era was Beethoven. As a whimsical thought experiment, imagine what it would mean to be able to teach in the way that Beethoven composed. When we can do that, Romanticism will truly have come of age.

Fourth, I would say that anthroposophy, by whatever name one uses and practiced perhaps even by someone who has not heard of Rudolf Steiner, may be thought of as the informing discipline of our age, by which I mean the period that began with the scientific revolution of the late sixteenth and seventeenth centuries and gave rise to our modern minds, mindset, mentality, and consciousness.

In contrast, philosophy, developed during Classical Greek times, was the informing discipline of the previous age. Philosophy split over time into theology ("the Queen of the Sciences"), "natural philosophy," which we now simply call science, and all the other disciplines that we study in universities. (An exception to this is history, which arose in Greece at the same time as philosophy, and which has been its constant companion ever since.) Philosophy is, of course, still worthy of study, but we could say that it is far less vital than it used to be. For instance, Richard Rorty, the renowned American philosopher, left the field for literature studies, believing philosophy as a study has run its course.

Yet in what sense do I mean that anthroposophy is the informing discipline of our times? I mean that it aims consciously to overcome our division of the world into subject and object, inner and outer, quality and quantity. We will maintain these distinctions, but, as Steiner demonstrates in his *Philosophy of Freedom*, we also recognize increasingly that these divisions arise subsequent to our consciousness of the world. The initial source of this division of the world, which, in each life currently occurs in us at so young an age that we are unaware of it, is revived in what Steiner occasionally called living thinking, which Barfield called "concrete" thinking, and which Henri Bortoft has called "upstream" thinking.

Fifth, and finally, I will add Barfield's description of anthroposophy: "Anthroposophy is knowledge as it is expressed and grasped by the Consciousness Soul." To put this another way, anthroposophy is knowledge as it is expressed and grasped by those who are inwardly free. Despite—or because of—the challenges of the fragmented, relativistic, reductionistic, mechanistic modern mind, human beings are, potentially, inwardly free in a way that they have not been in prior times.

To conclude this chapter, I would like to quote Barfield one final time:

> To become an anthroposophist is not to believe, it is to decide to use the words of Rudolf Steiner (and any others which may become available) for the purpose of raising oneself, if possible, to a kind of thinking which is itself beyond words. This is that concrete thinking [or living thinking; neither subjective nor objective but thinking prior to this division] which is the source of all such ideas and propositions, the source of all meaning whatsoever. ("Speech, Reason, and Imagination" in *Romanticism Comes of Age*)

PRINCIPLES

25. BEYOND MYTH-BUSTING: UNDERSTANDING OUR EVOLVING RELATIONSHIP TO RUDOLF STEINER'S EDUCATIONAL WORK IN THE PAST, THE PRESENT, AND THE FUTURE

Rudolf Steiner said many things about teaching, learning, and child development. Over time, these have informed what we call and what we have created as Waldorf or Steiner education. We have adopted some of the practices Steiner recommended and we have not adopted others. In addition, we have adopted practices about which Steiner said nothing or against which Steiner spoke specifically.

In considering our work in the present and planning our work for the future, we would do well to examine our teaching practices in light of what Steiner said and didn't say, what we currently do and don't do, and what we might or might not do in the future. This way of looking at our work can help us move beyond an entrenched or dogmatic view. More importantly, it honors an educational method that of necessity is alive and constantly evolving.

Much work has been done in the past ten or fifteen years in what we may call "myth-busting," attempting to demonstrate the ways in which what we call Waldorf education are occasionally at odds with Rudolf Steiner's intentions for educational practice.[15]

My own interest in the topic dates back, in part, to the differences in practice that I observed in moving from the Waldorf School of Garden City, which I had attended as a student and at which I taught for twelve years, to the Great Barrington Rudolf Steiner School, where I was a teacher and administrator for five years before moving to the Berkshire Waldorf High School. The Waldorf School of Garden City, founded in 1947, had no "math gnomes" or "circle time" because these practices evolved somewhat later and at other schools. Each school develops and carries its own culture and practices. Over time, of course, schools cross-pollinate, and I'm sure circle time and even math gnomes have found their way to some Garden City classrooms.

Meanwhile, to assist consideration, I created the following matrix that lays out the logical possibilities for engaging with what Steiner said—or didn't say. It includes what we do now and what we might do in the future. A plus sign (+) indicates an educational practice that Steiner advocated, something we currently practice, or something we might practice in the future. A minus sign (–) indicates an educational practice about which Steiner is silent, one we currently do not practice, or one we will not practice in the future.

	Past: Steiner said... or he didn't...	Present: We do... or we don't...	Future: We will... or we will not...
1	+	+	+
2	+	+	–
3	+	–	+
4	+	–	–
5	–	–	–
6	–	–	+
7	–	+	–
8	–	+	+

Table 1. *Educational practices, based in the work of Rudolf Steiner, of the past, present, and future*

Although this table may appear at first to be somewhat abstract, I believe it presents a more thoughtful and sophisticated way to think about what we do in Waldorf schools—and how it evolves—than simple references to "Steiner said" or "Steiner never said." Instead of an adversarial conversation about what we should or shouldn't do, it helps us situate our present practice within its origins in the past and its possibilities for the future.

This matrix and the thinking behind it are intended to be a tool for structured conversations in schools and among colleagues regarding their teaching practices. Participants don't need to have a logical diagram in hand; they just need to be aware of and remain open to the possibilities laid out here.

I will consider all eight possibilities, with illustrative examples. My examples are not necessarily yours. But, as you'll see, the thinking behind each follows a pattern that imbues it with value. Even if you disagree with my examples and conclusions, you and I can discuss where you believe I went wrong, we can present evidence, and we can arrive at a considered opinion that, with some work, takes us beyond mere assertions of agreement or disagreement.

Each of the eight possibilities arrayed in my matrix is not equally worthy of our time. Some practices clearly derive from Steiner's work, are central to our practice, and should continue into the future relatively unquestioned. For instance, the first row is the least problematic. Steiner recommended a practice, we employ it, and we agree to continue to employ it in the future:

Example of Row 1 in the table:

> **Past:** Steiner said we should teach imaginatively for students between the ages of seven and fourteen.
> **Present:** We are doing this. It's one of the greatest strengths of our current practice and the reason many parents send their children to us and teachers find value in their work.
> **Future:** We should continue doing this.

Although the first row may be in some ways the least problematic, it is also likely the home of the more profound and essential aspects of what we do. Education imbued with spirituality? Developmentally appropriate education? Teaching that addresses an image of a triune human being? Education for environmental reverence and social health? We agree on these, try to practice them, and don't need a lot of conversation to agree to continue to address them in the future. The challenge here is not to question practice but to deepen it.

Row 2 asks the question of what are we doing today, based on Steiner's work, that we should not do tomorrow? If we understand Steiner to have asked for teaching that is alienating or racist, for example, and if we are currently teaching in this mode, then we should consider abandoning it. Such considerations belong in this row. Abandoning a practice recommended by Steiner is not something Waldorf schools or teachers should do lightly, but if we are honest, we must admit its possibility.

Example of Row 2:

> Past: Some of Steiner's remarks about, say, the French
> and the French language are incendiary, to say the
> least.[16]
>
> Present: Teachers who base their attitude toward
> the French and the French language on Steiner's
> remarks would be highly and inappropriately
> prejudiced.
>
> Future: Any such teachers should strongly consider
> altering their practice in the future. Schools that
> employ them may have to censure their work.

Row 3 points us toward engaging with suggestions
Steiner made for teaching but that we have not made part
of our practice. Nearly each time I teach a course, even
one I have taught twenty or more times, I return to Stockmeyer's *Curriculum* to reread the relevant section. I almost
always find something new, something I don't recall reading before, something I can use to refresh my teaching and
make it better and more effective. If necessary, I don't stop
with Stockmeyer, but head directly for the Steiner work to
which Stockmeyer refers. I believe a significant portion of
our math, history, and science teaching would be improved
by attention to considerations of this type. But here is an
example from painting:

Example of Row 3:

> Past: In *Practical Advice to Teachers* (p. 35), Steiner
> said that painting on both white and colored or
> tinted paper would have an enlivening effect on
> students.
>
> Present: Many teachers do not do this and may not
> even be aware of this recommendation.

Future: We should strongly consider making it part of
our practice in the future.

In my view, Steiner was wrong about some things. He
was human and fallible. These simple statements may be
considered heretical by some of my colleagues, but not to
admit them is to insult both Steiner's humanity and the possibility for the growth and development of our teaching
practice. Further, not to admit to them is to add to a sec-
tarian and isolationist view of Steiner and anthroposophy.
Even if you and I are not capable of saying precisely where
Steiner was incorrect, we must admit the existence of his
errors. The fourth line of my matrix considers practices that
Steiner may have advocated but that we do not implement
and should not implement in the future.

Before giving the following example, however, it should
be noted that Steiner was not, in this instance, advocating
the correction of left-handedness *for writing*, and that he
did not advocate changing left-handedness in all or even
most circumstances. But this example has been used to
claim that Steiner was in favor of consistent changing of
left-handedness. This situation points to the need for vigi-
lance in accepting claims of "Steiner said," the need to check
the source and the context, and the need to apply sound
judgment to the specific circumstance. This includes the possibility that Steiner was wrong.

Example of Row 4:

Past: On page 345 of *Faculty Meetings with Rudolf
Steiner,* vol. 1, Steiner said, and perhaps said elsewhere, "We should always correct left-handedness."
Present: Research shows that asking children
to switch hands may often have deleterious

consequences, and many, if not most, teachers do not attempt this.

Future: We should continue strongly to question switching children from left-handedness to right-handedness. Steiner was principally concerned with ambidextrous children when he advocated emphasizing right-handedness for writing, and any orthodoxy here can easily do more harm than good.

Row 5 considers practices that were, are, and should remain outside our practice.

Example of Row 5:

Past: Steiner did not advocate corporal punishment.
Present: We do not indulge corporal punishment.
Future: We should not consider corporal punishment.

Row 6 is perhaps the most challenging row of all. It suggests areas of practice for which we cannot turn to Steiner for reference, as he did not speak on them, areas in which we currently are not practicing, but areas in which we will be called to practice in the future. To successfully meet these demands of the future, we will have to take the reins that Steiner (and others) have given us, so to speak. Here we may develop the imagination and intuition to deal creatively, ethically, and freely with the as-yet-unknown. This is, in fact, the area for which anthroposophy prepares us. We should face the challenges in this area with courage, renewed commitment, and vigor. We might imagine that considerations that belong in this row exist only in the future, but I believe my example shows that they are clearly already here.

Example of Row 6:

Past: To my knowledge, although Steiner spoke about the effects of alcohol, narcotics, and other substances, he didn't say anything about many of the drugs, including marijuana, that our students may abuse.

Present: Beyond some prohibitive policies that seem to have more to do with our current comfort and practical considerations than with educational ideals, we, too, frequently don't contend with the implications of our students' drug use.

Future: We should probably develop a more insightful, thoughtful education around student drug use.

And, finally, in rows 7 and 8, we find the examples of "myths" that prompted my thinking about this topic, practices that have evolved since Steiner lived and that we must examine carefully to determine if they are valuable or, rather, if they have become baseless and dogmatic.

Example of Row 7:

Past: Steiner did not say we should use "math gnomes" to teach math.

Present: We frequently use math gnomes to teach math in the early elementary grades.

Future: We should stop using math gnomes to teach math. They trivialize the elemental world and sidestep Steiner's own suggestions for math teaching.

Example of Row 8:

Past: Steiner did not say students should gather for "circle time" in the morning.

Present: Students currently gather for circle time, which seems to have been introduced to schools, including Waldorf schools, in the late 1970s or 1980s.

Future: Students should continue to gather for circle time, as appropriate. After all, to gather in a circle is a powerful social force. So long as work in a circle reinforces or assists learning and the purpose of the morning lesson, it is clearly a healthful practice.

To end with another, more complex example, take the prohibition on the use of black in young children's drawings and paintings. Although Steiner did not offer a prescription or prohibition with regard to the use of black in children's work, it is possible to interpret his work to justify this prohibition. The challenge is to keep this policy healthy and relevant. If we simply adopt it without understanding it, we become dogmatists and immediately subvert our own aims to create a living method of education.

Implementing ideas dogmatically also causes all kinds of practical and cultural problems. For example, removing black but leaving brown and pink in a box of crayons allows those children with pink skin and brown hair to draw their likeness, while brown-skinned children with black hair are stymied. This is a horror, especially in the United States, given our history of slavery and racism. Thoughtful teachers will not indulge a prohibition on black, but may healthfully choose to give children only prismatic colors ("rainbow" colors), removing not only the black but also the colors that allow any children to draw naturally-colored skin or hair.

Further, as a thought experiment, imagine you are teaching children in impoverished circumstances. You have charcoal with which you may draw, and nothing else. Is it better to forego drawing altogether, or to use the charcoal, even though it's black?

Conversations along these lines, conversations that begin with research and a clear understanding of Steiner's educational work and that take into account current practices and their validity and efficacy, will clarify our work in schools and move us toward ever better teaching and learning.

Finally, however, these conversations can go only as deep as the persons having them are capable of going. It is incumbent on each one of us to continue our development as human beings through contemplative, reflective practice and through warm, honest relationships with each other. Only increasingly human teachers will honor Rudolf Steiner's educational aims and honor the humanity of the students they teach.

✤

26. POLARITIES:
THE VALUABLE ACT OF IMAGINATION

You stand outside a burning building. A loved one is trapped inside. You are afraid. And if you cannot overcome your fear, you will watch your loved one perish.

You stand outside a burning building. A loved one is trapped inside. You must resist the urge to rush thoughtlessly, foolishly into the building. If you cannot resist your foolhardiness, you and your loved one will both perish.

You stand outside a burning building. A loved one is trapped inside. If you can act courageously, overcoming fear and withstanding the urge to rash action, you may save your loved one.

In human experience, then, courage is not some interaction between adrenaline and electrochemical neurology. It is that capacity that can arise when we allow fear and foolhardiness to "interpenetrate" within us. A courageous person experiences fear, and she also feels the impulse to act without thinking. She is able, however, to maintain a dynamic tension between these forces of fear and foolhardiness, and, in mediating them, to act courageously. The opposition of fear and foolhardiness, the polarity between them, provides the possibility for courage to arise.

Apologies for the melodramatic opening. But part of the challenge in writing about polarities is that the writing can come off as dry and logical, when the phenomena of polar interactions are so alive, multifaceted, and interesting. It's the difference between describing an optical demonstration in which a prism is interposed between a beam of light and a projector screen and the experience of seeing the rainbow of colors that results.

Many thinkers, from Heraclitus and Plato to Goethe and Steiner to Yeats and James Joyce, have found value in demonstrating how capacities, qualities, and values arise through the interaction of apparent opposites, polarities.

What is a polarity? It is an opposition or tension between two qualities or capacities that, in their "interpenetration" or "intensification" or "held balance" give rise to a third quality or capacity. In the words of Elaine Hocks, it is "a dynamic and generative interpenetration of opposites."

The interpenetration or intensification is dynamic, moving, we could even say "alive," although not in a strictly biological sense. The new creation of the interaction or mediated tension between the poles is never static or single.

The interaction of light and darkness, in the color theory brilliantly elaborated by Goethe, produces color—all color, from the dullest gray-brown to the most luminous, brilliant gold, with all hues and shades in between.

Similarly, Steiner's description of emotions arising from movement between attraction (sympathy) and repulsion (antipathy) shows how all emotions, from the gentlest glimmer of new love to the strongest expression of courage, arise from polar phenomena.

The emotion we call courage, the capacity for appropriate action in the face of fear and the tug of foolhardiness, fits within Steiner's more general polarity in which emotions arise out of attraction and repulsion. Fear repels us; we must face a fear to overcome it, and resist its repulsive force. Hence, perhaps, the allure of ghost stories and horror movies. And foolhardiness draws us toward rash action.

This gives some evidence of what we might call the "holographic nature" of polarities—one nested inside another. I leave it to you to decide whether or not all polarities are in the end nested in one grand one.

Similarly, the pole in one polarity may become the capacity developed by another. Thinking and perceiving form a powerful polarity from which consciousness arises, as Steiner, and Barfield demonstrate. But thinking itself is the result of a polarity, according to Barfield, between the "universalizing" and the "particularizing" movements of our minds.

This gives evidence of the "netlike" web of meaning that polarities inhabit. A polarity reveals or creates a quality or truth, but to fully comprehend its ends we must move to another polarity. This sounds like a call to relativism and a hall of mirrors, each point of meaning leading to another, not more meaningful or revealing than the last. It's difficult to move swiftly past this point, but suffice it to say that just because we may move from pole to pole does not mean that each polarity is equal in meaning or import.

One strange aspect of polar existence is that the central phenomenon—color, let's say, or emotions—can be experienced, used, and studied, often fruitfully, without understanding the polarity that gives rise to the phenomenon. But we could say that real understanding, the beginning of meaning, comes only with recognition of and experience of the polarity that gives rise to the phenomenon under investigation.

To think in polarities—to recognize their existence and their power and, particularly, to live in the moving, multidimensional creations of their resolution or in the balance of tension that they produce—is to think in a living way. This may not be the only thing that Steiner meant by "living thinking," but it is one.

It's entirely possible, by the way, to read my description of polarities, or someone else's—such as Barfield's or Coleridge's—to "understand" polarities in some academic or intellectual way, to be able to explain them to someone else, but not be able creatively or imaginatively to enter their existence. It takes human activity, an act of imagination, to enter the activity of polar phenomena. I find that my ability to contend with them flickers over time—sometimes I approach more closely; other times, I meet a wall of incomprehension. Do two phenomena that appear in opposition present a polarity? Only work over time—assisted by the research of others—will tell.

The concept of polarity...is not really a logical concept at all, but one which requires an act of imagination to grasp it.... Unlike the logical principles of identity and contradiction, it is not only a form of thought, but also the form of life. It could perhaps be called the principle of seminal identity. It is also the formal principle which underlies meaning itself and the expansion of meaning." (Owen Barfield, *Speaker's Meaning*, pp. 38–39)

In this sense, polarities are akin in some ways to proofs in formal geometry. A student of geometry can be led through the steps leading to a proof, but the "QED," the experience that these steps constitute a proof, arises only in the imaginative perception of the student. As a teacher, I can state and restate terms and relationships, trying to make clear that their relationship constitutes a proof, but only the student can generate the insight to leap over the intuitive gap presented by the final step of the proof and "see" the truth of the proof.

Similarly, an apparent opposition only becomes a generative polarity through an intuitive act of insight.

Further, a student can learn to repeat the words of a proof, uncomprehendingly, just as someone can repeat the words of, say, Goethe's demonstration of the polarity between light and darkness that gives rise to color, or Steiner's assertion that emotions arise from the interaction of antipathy and sympathy, without living in or comprehending the reality of this relationship. Barfield calls this "the intellectual soul masquerading as the consciousness soul."

And, once this relationship has been experienced, rather than simply reiterated, its truth is unshakably present, just as is the truth of a proof in geometry, once "seen." It may be re-experienced, almost at will, but it cannot be easily forgotten. To perceive a polarity changes the person who perceives it.

It's also clear that what we may describe in polarities is not necessarily what we mean when we describe something as "dialectical." Dialectics, in simplest form, is the famous conflict between thesis (statement), antithesis (counter-statement), and their resolution in synthesis (which becomes the new thesis). This wheel of oppositions may describe what occurs in the world—for example, slavery (thesis) and anti-slavery (antithesis) clash during the U.S. Civil War, and the antitheses include the end of slavery but the continuation of racism and oppression (synthesis). The new creation here is not the result of "interpenetration," "balance," or mediated, creative tension, but simply of strife. Dialectics may be powerful—in argument and in Marx's dialectical materialism—but it is a wheel that churns what already exists, not a creative process that gives rise to something new.

Coleridge used the language of dialectics to describe polarity, but added a critical condition:

> Every power in nature and in spirit must evolve an opposite as the sole means and condition of its manifestation: and all opposition is a tendency to re-union. This is the universal law of polarity or essential dualism, first promulgated by Heraclitus.... The principle may be thus expressed. The identity of thesis and antithesis is the substance of all being; their opposition the condition of all existence or being manifested: and every thing or phenomenon is the exponent of a synthesis *as long as the opposite energies are retained in that synthesis.* (S. T. Coleridge, quoted in E. D. Hocks, "Dialectic and the 'Two Forces of One Power': Reading Coleridge, Polanyi, and Bakhtin in a New Key," p. 5, italics added)

In every polarity, the possibility exists that the poles will simply be allowed to meet and mix, unmediated, unintensified, without interpenetrating. This "unmediated" mixture of poles does not produce any new third quality or value. Light and dark can simply swirl together to make shades of gray. Fear and foolhardiness can simply mix to produce anxiety or even panic. The simple mixture of thinking and will produces "false" or "dead" emotions. Here I think of C. S. Lewis's *Men Without Chests*. The mixture of thinking and perceiving results in a conventional consciousness, that Barfield calls, pejoratively, "common sense," and which includes the illusion of thinking accompanied by the illusion of perceiving. And beauty and meaning can mix to produce propaganda or advertising, a hollow shell or the illusion of art.

In each polarity, one pole tends to be more "active" and one more "passive" or "receptive." One accords more with cognition, the other with will or action.

The circumstance of a polarity offers three possibilities for error, then:

1. A failure to allow the ends of the polarity to interpenetrate, producing only the illusion, the gray, the base mixture, the apathetic, the conventional appearance of resolution.
2. Yielding to the temptation of one pole—fiery egocentricity, warmth, beauty, perception, sympathy, foolishness, and light. And:
3. Yielding to the temptation of the other pole—despair, meaninglessness, cold abstraction and intellect, antipathy, and darkness.

And the human being who stands between these, allowing them to interpenetrate in thinking and perceiving, must rouse herself to (inner) activity to resolve the tension between them, to allow them to interpenetrate.

Polarities are contextual and situational, and all three "parts" of them seem to arise simultaneously. For instance, antipathy does not exist until its opposite, sympathy, is also present, and both spring into being with the feeling between them. We may imagine light and darkness sitting around, waiting (to be separated one from the other), and then color arising sometime later through their interaction. But, of course, we see color first and only in imagination perceive the generative poles of light and darkness. In schematizing a polarity, we may imagine the poles existing "first" and determining the creative intensification arising "later," but, in reality, all three spring into being at the same time. We could say that someone who too literally sketches polarities in an abstract way simply doesn't quite understand what he is talking about—or understands it superficially without actually living it.

Some values or qualities are not immediately obvious as poles, but resolve into a polarity when properly apprehended. Goethe's work on color is obviously, incontrovertibly true within its conceptual framework to anyone who has studied it and understood or apprehended it, and yet it's still controversial—seen as a matter of "belief" by those who know "about" it but do not *know* it.

In the growth or development of a human, we may move from one to the other—will in youth, thinking in old age, for example. In human history, too, we may move from a more perceptive consciousness to a more cognitive consciousness. It's more complicated than this, but I'm trying to keep this brief. In general, polarities present not a static creation, but one that moves. And this movement may have a meaningful direction in a human life or in the life of the world.

Not every pair of apparent opposites is necessarily a polarity. Good and evil, for example, don't "interpenetrate" to produce a third quality or value. To paraphrase C.S. Lewis, this is because evil is simply fallen or twisted good, derivative of good, not its opposite.

Finally, a polarity is not a duality, and consideration of polarities does not perpetuate another dualistic philosophy. In fact, polarities are simultaneously both whole (one) and "triune," and they provide a path—possibly the only path— away from dualism and irreconcilable "two-realm" theories of truth.

I will end with some examples of polarities that I have collected over the past couple of years.

1. For Plato, in the dialogue *Laches*, and, more explicitly, for Aristotle in Book 2 of *Nicomachean Ethics*, courage is the "mean" or mediated interaction or interpenetration between fear (too much thinking that precludes action) and foolhardiness (action that is not tempered by thought). I have used this as my entry to thinking about polarities at the beginning of this chapter. Plato, however, does not use the word *polarity*. He is not didactic, and the dialogue, as a whole, presents in a living way what I have made a bit more cut-and-dried here.

2. In his *Theory of Colors*, Goethe showed that color arises as the interpenetration of light and dark. Darkness seen through a light-filled medium, atmosphere or prism, appears as cyan, blue, or violet. Light seen through a dense medium, atmosphere or prism, appears as red, orange, or yellow.

3. Plant growth and development can be seen as a living process that occurs between the poles of expansion and contraction, as Goethe demonstrated in his *Metamorphosis of Plants*.

4. Steiner showed how the polarity of cognition (antipathy) and will (sympathy) in a human soul gives rise to feelings or emotions. Feelings lead us to put our thoughts into action; feelings likewise lead us to think about our actions. The words *sympathy* and *antipathy* are challenging in English—sympathy seems "good," antipathy "bad"—and Steiner did not mean them to have these shades of meaning. Both are necessary, and the tension between them is also necessary. We might better talk about something that attracts us and something that distances us. Each is appropriate in its proper sphere.

5. Barfield, following Steiner, shows how thinking and perceiving give rise to human consciousness. We can think about the world, and we can perceive the world. Both arise simultaneously in us, producing consciousness. There is (despite William James's thought experiment about a "blooming, buzzing confusion" or Merleau-Ponty's hypothesis regarding the "primacy of perception") no pure or prime perception; no perception without thought, and vice versa. Each discovers itself in the other, in consciousness.

6. For this example, I will quote Joseph Campbell:

> James Joyce, in *A Portrait of the Artist as a Young Man*, makes a distinction between what he calls "proper art" and "improper art." By "proper art" he means that which really belongs to art. "Improper art," by contrast, is art that's in the service of something that is not art: for instance, art in the service of advertising. Further, referring to the attitude of the observer, Joyce says that proper art is static, and

thereby induces esthetic arrest, whereas improper art is kinetic, filled with movement: meaning, it moves you to desire or to fear and loathing. Art that excites desire for the object as a tangible object he calls pornographic. Art that excites loathing or fear for the object he terms didactic, or instructive. All sociological art is didactic. Most novels since Zola's time have been the work of didactic pornographers, who are preaching a social doctrine of some kind and fancying it up with pornographic icing. Say you are leafing through a magazine and see an advertisement for a beautiful refrigerator. There's a girl with lovely refrigerating teeth smiling beside it, and you say, "I'd love to have a refrigerator like that." That ad is pornography. By definition, all advertising art is pornographic art. (Joseph Campbell, *Reflections on the Art of Living*, p. 246)

We can summarize this in a polarity between sensuality and dry meaning: Pornography is beauty or sensuality without meaning; pedantry is meaning without beauty or sensuality. If we think of beauty and meaning as a polarity, their interpenetration, both beautiful and meaningful, is art.

7. And another quotation, now of a poem:

Things fall apart. The center cannot hold....
The best lack all conviction while the worst
Are full of passionate intensity.
    (William Butler Yeats, "The Second Coming")

"Lacking all conviction" refers to giving in to meaningless ego denial; "passionate intensity" describes the temptation of egocentricity. The polarity between too much ego and not enough ego is resolved in the healthy self.

8. Michael D'Aleo demonstrates (I won't give away the secret of precisely how) that our apprehension of material objects in the world requires the interaction of two senses—touch and sight. We see things that are not objects—the colors at sunset, for example—and we feel things that are not objects—the wind at our back, for example. Only when our sight and touch corroborate each other do we create the concept of and perceive tangible, physical, material objects. Our visual field is built, in large measure, of the tangible, and we conceptualize the world as a unity based on the interaction of these two senses.

☙

27. How to Ruin the Soul of the Child

Translations of Quotations Taken out of Context from Rudolf Steiner

I would like to attempt to make sense of Steiner's frequent references to "soul ruining," some of which are collected below. As a first pass at attempting to say, in part, what Steiner may have meant by "soul ruining," we may turn to a 2011 item on NPR's *Planet Money*.[17] Job training, it turns out, is more effective for those who have had an early childhood education, controlled for socioeconomic variables. Nobel-prize-winning economist James Heckman found that training relies on what he calls "soft skills," which "involve things like being able to pay attention and focus, being curious and open to new experiences, and being able to control your temper and not get frustrated," things you learn in preschool. Astonishingly, on average, boys who went to preschool, in one study, were found to be fifty percent less likely to be in jail, and to earn fifty percent more than their peers. Further, skills not learned early are harder and harder—and ultimately impossible—to learn later. Doesn't it seem possible—adjusting for translation from an early twentieth century German idiom, expressed in lectures transcribed later—that the souls of one group were less "ruined," in an early twenty-first century, non-judgmental way, than the souls of the others?

Now for the Steiner quotations:

> Conclusions can live and be healthy only in the living human spirit. That is, the conclusion is healthy only when it exists in completely conscious life. That is very important, as we will see later. For that reason, you ruin children's souls if you have the children memorize finished conclusions. (*Foundations of Human Experience*, p. 150)

> Proceed to reflect with the children, without hesitation, that you are looking beyond their horizon. It does not matter, you see, if you say a great deal to the children that they will understand only later. The principle that dictates that you teach the children only what they can understand and form an opinion about has ruined much in our culture. (Ibid., pp. 48–49)

> You can present the human intellect, in a makeshift way, with historical or physiological facts before age twelve, but by doing so you ruin human nature; strictly speaking, you make it unsuitable for the whole of life. (Ibid., p. 110)

> Do not give children verbal definitions but show them the connections between the concepts and the phenomena related to air and those related to solid bodies. Once we have grasped the concept of solid bodies flowing in

the direction in which they tend when not prevented, we can dispense with the concept of air flowing into empty space. Healthier concepts would arise than those that fill the world today—such as Professor Einstein's complicated theory of relativity. I mention this as a passing comment on the present state of our civilization, for I cannot avoid pointing out how many harmful ideas live in our culture (such as the theory of relativity, especially in its most recent variation). These ideas run a ruinous course if the child becomes a research scientist. (Ibid., p. 117)

By using shorthand, we retain something in our culture that, if left to ourselves with our present natural aptitudes, we would cease to notice and, in fact, forget. We thus keep something artificially awake in our culture that destroys it just as much as all-night studying ruins the health of overzealous students. For this reason, our culture is no longer truly healthy. (Ibid., p. 132)

The children do not as yet have a full understanding for matters of the rights sphere, and if they are confronted with these concepts too early in their development, their soul forces will be ruined for the rest of their lives because such concepts will be so abstract. (Ibid., p. 151)

Thus, because of this method of treatment—giving him wine as a young child—he was completely ruined by the time he was seven years old. (*Discussion with Teachers*, p. 105)

Experimental psychology can be a valuable basis of psychology, but when it sneaks into pedagogy and even into courtrooms, it ruins everything that requires healthy development, that needs fully developed people not separated by a gulf from other fully developed people. (Ibid., p. 150)

We must not understand our task as imagining that what is good for one is good for everyone, since thinking so abstractly would be the ruin of all genuine desire. (Ibid., p. 162)

For the convenience of the faculty, the child has, for instance, mathematics or arithmetic in the first period; then, perhaps Latin, then, maybe a period of religion. After that, there is music or singing, but maybe not even that, and, instead, geography. We cannot more fundamentally ruin human nature than by teaching children in this manner. (*Education as a Force for Social Change*, p. 168)

The first thing you have to do is to dispense with all the textbooks. For textbooks as they are written at the present time contain nothing about the plant and animal kingdoms that we can use in teaching. They are good for instructing grown-up people about plants and animals, but you will ruin the individuality of the child if you use them at school. (Ibid., p. 37)

The chief point is that thinking must never, never be separated from visual experience, from what the children can see, for otherwise intellectualism and abstractions are brought to the children in early life and thereby ruin their whole being. The children will become dried up and this will affect not only the soul life but the physical body also, causing desiccation and sclerosis. (Ibid., p. 84)

Now if there is the right treatment in the language lessons, that is to say if the teacher does not ruin the child's feeling for language but rather cherishes it, then the child will feel the transition to eurythmy to be a perfectly natural one, just as the very little child feels that learning to speak is also a perfectly natural process. (*The Kingdom of Childhood*, p. 105)

Children should not enter elementary school before their seventh year. I was always glad to hear, therefore (and I don't mind if you consider this uncivilized), that the children of some anthroposophists had no knowledge of writing and reading, even at the age of eight. Accomplishments that come with forces that are available later on should never be forced into an earlier stage, unless we are prepared to ruin the physical organism. (Ibid., p. 116)

Through ill treatment, a violin may be ruined forever. But in the case of the living human organism, it is possible to plant principles that are harmful to growth, which increase and develop until they eventually ruin a person's entire life. (Ibid., p. 137)

We ruin our students' future worldviews when we introduce them prematurely to subjects such as chemistry, mineralogy, physics, dynamics, and so on. (Ibid., p. 192)

People prefer to fall back on traditional religious creeds, trying to bridge what remains unbridgeable unless they can rise from the sensory world to the spiritual world, as anthroposophy endeavors to do. For adults, such a conflict is indeed tragic. If it arises in childhood before the eleventh year, it brings disturbances in its wake that are serious enough to ruin the soul life of a child. A child should never have to say, "I study zoology and find nothing about God. It's true that I hear of God when I study religion, but this does not help explain zoology." To allow children to be caught in such a dilemma would be awful, since this kind of questioning can completely throw them off their proper course in life. (*Soul Economy*, p. 281)

At about the age of twelve, while still under the guidance of authority, another important desire, namely, to reason independently, begins to develop. If we use independent reasoning too much before the age of twelve, we will actually ruin the child's soul and bodily forces. In a certain sense, we deaden human experiencing with reason. (*The Renewal of Education*, p. 135)

GOVERNANCE AND ADMINISTRATION

28. THREEFOLD SOCIAL ORGANIZATION AND WALDORF SCHOOL GOVERNANCE

According to Rudolf Steiner, social organizations should have three cooperative but independent administrations—one to administer economic functions, one to administer rights and responsibilities of members of the organization, and one to administer what he calls the organization's "spiritual" or "cultural" functions—he uses these words interchangeably in discussions of social questions.[18] These three administrations scale to cover the smallest institutions and the largest social groups. One administration may consider itself more central than the others to the mission of a particular organization, but all must balance if the organization is to maintain itself in health. A school, for instance, could mirror a theocracy if educational concerns are used to trump or bully the genuine concerns of the rights of its consumers.

This example points to the intuitive correctness of Steiner's view. Take the opposite view: Do we believe that justice should be bought and sold, or that the state should govern religion? For those seeking a more conventional (but no less difficult to comprehend) statement of a view of the threefold structure of society, Jurgen Habermas's concept of a "lifeworld," discussed in detail in the second volume of his *Theory of Communicative Action*, outlines a view that is essentially the same as Steiner's. For Habermas, every communicative act—asking a question, making a statement—expresses all three of the human subsystems of thinking, feeling, and will. (That is, the most rigorous thought is still communicated with some emotional investment and some intention of will, and the most emotional outburst still gives evidence of a thought and an intention.) Further, every communicative act, in that it is directed from one person to another or to a group of others, extends the human capacities of thinking, feeling, and will into a social interaction. Thinking extended into social interaction we may call culture; feeling extended becomes politics; and will extended concerns economic relations.

For Steiner, an economic administration should function according to a principle of solidarity (Steiner says "brotherhood," but we should update this) through an "association of producers, distributors, and consumers." For a school, a child's education is a product in the economic sphere. It is more than this, but it is also this. Hence, a school should have an administrative body that is comprised of producers—representatives of teachers and staff—and consumers—representatives of the parent body as proxies for their children. Such an administration, to ensure that its work is legal and effective, will also require legal and financial expertise. (Introducing expertise of any kind, we should acknowledge, introduces something from the spiritual-cultural sphere.)

The work of this administration is to balance the needs, desires, and resources of producers and consumers to produce a budget and plan for the future. Clearly, this administrative body may be identified with a school's board of trustees.

An administration of the spiritual-cultural area of a school functions according to a principle of freedom, and so, despite tradition and received wisdom, it is difficult if not impossible to say how this administration will or should be governed. It might operate as a so-called College of Teachers that uses a consensus decision-making model, but, in freedom, there is no requirement that it do so.

Steiner did not specify a decision-making process for cultural organizations (and, if he did, we would still have to decide for ourselves whether or not we agree with his statements), and, in fact, in the meetings to reorganize the Anthroposophical Society in 1923–24, he stated that the process mattered little and should be left up to individual groups. One group might choose to function aristocratically, another more democratically. His position was that the structure mattered less than the persons involved, and that those chosen to carry out a task be given the freedom to do it. I believe his views here are directly applicable to constituting the administration of a Waldorf school. And, in the first Waldorf school, Steiner was the director, appointed by acclamation, not by vote.

A spiritual-cultural administration consists of the teachers in the school, regardless of how they structure their governance or decision-making. As Steiner said, "no one who is not a teacher is to have anything to say [about how education is conducted]." Powerful words, if true. Of course, visiting teachers—consultants, mentors—and doctors and therapists who work with the students in a school may be included. But that's about it. In a Waldorf school we may call this group the College of Teachers, the Core Faculty, the Council, or something else. We may worry that it is too small and too exclusive (and then work to make it larger and more inclusive), but this is the body in most Waldorf schools that corresponds to the free administration of the spiritual-cultural life of a school. And the work of this administration is the education of students.

A third administration, an administration of rights and responsibilities, which functions democratically according to a principle of equality, should clearly include representatives of every constituency of the school community, anyone who has any rights within the organization, anyone who has any responsibilities to the organization. Here we include students, parents, teachers, staff, alumni, retired faculty and staff, and even donors. All have some number of rights and responsibilities to the organism of the school. These include legally recognized rights, and so this administration requires legal representation, if not at every meeting, at least as an on-call resource.[19]

Rights are myriad. Perhaps they begin with clear, legally recognized rights, but they also include the policies and procedures of the school. Among other things, for instance, applicants have a right to a clear response to their application in a reasonable time. Responsibilities, too, are myriad. Parents must pay their bills. Teachers must engage in appropriate professional development. Breach of rights or responsibilities is reason for discipline or termination.

Policies, procedures, working conditions, and contracts all belong to this administration. Its work is to set and negotiate the boundaries within which the human beings in the organization conduct their work.

Often, it seems, this work is fragmented in Waldorf schools and is not given to one administration. The Board sets its own policies and procedures, as does the College of Teachers or Council. The support or administrative staff may do the same. A Human Resources committee may assume responsibility for some aspects of this work.

This fragmentation may lead to confusion and miscommunication among parents, teachers, and board members. Dysfunction in this area seems to plague Waldorf schools, and I would say that this happens, in part, because schools are clear about the function of a Board and a College but remarkably unclear about the function of this third administration—in fact, there is usually no single name we can use to designate it in a Waldorf school, and no single administrative body that consists of representatives of all the constituencies of the school.

In many schools, the Board sees this administration as part of its legal function, but then micromanages it—or fails to constitute and empower a committee that can take full responsibility for it, or fails to distinguish properly between economic concerns and those of rights and responsibilities. Similarly, Colleges of Teachers may fail to distinguish their appropriate educational function from that of a separate rights and responsibilities administration.

Schools would undoubtedly be stronger if there was a single administrative team, constituted according to correct principles, that oversaw this work. As it is, policies are too often weak or incomplete, forgotten or ignored, or simply absent, sending persons of otherwise good will up a wall and out of a school.

As a test case, we might ask first about a clear process for terminating a teacher who is not fulfilling her responsibilities to her students or the school. Schools accomplish this, but often with far greater ill will and rancor than sister institutions that do not claim to have such an idealistic view of the world but function with better management and clarity. And as a second test case, we might ask about a clear process and procedure for terminating this person if she is the Faculty Chair or other person who might otherwise be central to the termination of another colleague. Is there a safety valve or a back door?

Democracy here does not imply voting, or at least not voting alone. Dewey's broad definition of democracy as "conjoint community" may point us in the right direction. Decision-making may be democratic and consensus-driven (within legal boundaries), or it may be representational and use some other decision-making process. The point is that all voices are heard and considered.

⚜

29. YOU CAN'T ALWAYS GET WHAT YOU WANT: WALDORF SCHOOL ADMINISTRATION AND ENROLLMENT

Are 150 students, to pick a number, a good enrollment or a bad enrollment for an independent Waldorf elementary school?[20]

Among other factors, it depends on your point of view.

As a school grows from 100 to 120 and, finally, to 150, 150 feels like a comfortable number, a sustainable number, a number worth celebrating. The budget is balanced. Maybe there's even a small surplus to create a reserve or put toward deferred maintenance or a capital campaign.

But if a school has 200 students and then sees its enrollment drop to 180, 160, and then to 150, it may feel as if the sky is falling and that the school is on the verge of collapse.

The schools may have the same buildings, the same classrooms, the same playgrounds and fields, even the same teachers...yet totally different feelings. So, beyond the worry of declining enrollment, what's different? The ways in which a growing school structures itself to serve 150 students may be very different from the ways in which a shrinking school does the same thing.

Often, I believe, a large part of this difference lies in administration and support staff. Many shrinking Waldorf schools will cut teachers—full-time music or handwork or eurythmy teachers can be cut back to part-time—before they cut staff. They believe that they "have to have" an admissions director, a development director, a full-time administrator, and so on. Nothing against anyone in these positions—I've been married to a spectacular fundraiser for almost twenty-seven years and I've been a school administrator for thirteen years—but many Waldorf schools have an administrative staff that could support twice its actual enrollment or more.

In the end, however, a school's value lies in its education, in the quality of its programs, not in its administration.

How much less money would your school raise without your development director? What if she were half-time instead of full-time? Chances are, in a small school, that your community gives because it values the school and that its giving capacity doesn't cover the increased expense of a professional fundraiser.

Or, how many checks enter and leave the school in a month? A few dozen? How many hours do your business manager and bookkeeper really require? Plenty of efficient bookkeepers and business managers make a good living by working for several businesses, each for a few hours per week. But a job can expand to fill the hours allotted to it.

And how many admissions inquiries are there in a year at your school? How many tours? How many phone calls? Do you need a full-time admissions director? Do you even need a half-time admissions director?

Finally, is your administrator a teacher? If not, what do you make of Steiner's injunction below—one, incidentally, of remarkably few on the subject?

> The administration of the educational institutions, the organization of courses of instruction and their goals should be entirely in the hands of persons who themselves are *simultaneously* either teaching or otherwise productively engaged in cultural life. In each case, such persons would divide their time between actual teaching (or some other form of cultural productivity) and the administrative control of the educational system. It will be evident to anyone who can bring himself to an unbiased examination of cultural life that the peculiar vitality and energy of soul required for organizing and directing educational institutions will be called forth only in someone actively engaged in teaching or in some sort of cultural creativity. (Steiner, "The Threefold Social Order and Educational Freedom")

Or this one:

Teachers should arrange their time so that they can also be administrators in their fields. They should be just as at home attending to administrative matters as they are in the classroom. No one should make decisions who is not directly engaged in the educational process. No parliament or congress, nor any individual who was perhaps once an educator, is to have anything to say. (Steiner, *Towards Social Renewal*, p. 12)

I don't know exactly when and how the idea of a non-teaching administrator entered the world of Waldorf schools—probably sometime in the 1980s, and not at first, I believe, in the older or more established schools. But the introduction of a non-teaching administrator may not be a good idea.

And, similarly, based on an understanding of Steiner's insight, I question some of the activities of those in the Association of Waldorf Schools of North America (AWSNA) who no longer teach but who exercise control over the organization or direction of Waldorf schools!

I know from personal experience how quickly—and how subtly—I can lose touch with students once I step out of the classroom. I left teaching for about three years while I completed my doctorate, and I can still recall how I "lost my chops" with regard to my students. Yet I also recall, fortunately, how quickly my chops returned once I stepped back into the classroom. But, for that period when I was not teaching, advice I may have had to give toward teaching or school administration would have been theoretical and impractical, not based in reality and direct experience.[21]

Also, some schools have a dedicated but somewhat insecure board of trustees who may work against a "reality-based" view of school administration. These people may not know much about school management or function, let alone the peculiarities of Waldorf school management or function, let alone any type of small, underfunded, creative independent school management or function. Many trustees are somewhat uncertain when it comes to Steiner's work, and may follow the lead of the teachers who, in a worst-case scenario, misunderstand Steiner's work themselves and introduce ideology, belief, and dogma where it doesn't belong. Trustees may also work in businesses that don't operate so close to the bone and don't face the hard choices Waldorf schools sometimes need to make.

I can say, from experience, that the best board members are often small business owners who have built their businesses themselves. They are dogged, creative, entrepreneurial, and penny-pinching. They are reality-based, not theory-based. This is exactly what many schools need.

So, let's go back to the beginning and ask some questions. For starters, what administrative structure and configuration of full-time, part-time, and volunteer teaching and support did a school have the first year it joyfully reached an enrollment of 150? And that worked, right? And didn't everyone feel good? So why shouldn't a school that sees its enrollment drop to 150 recreate that original structure, rather than stagger along with a structure that it can't really support?

The school will have to do this less joyfully, but the structure will be based on a realistic plan that works, and it may provide a stronger platform for future growth.

Yet the question not addressed above is this: Why is your enrollment shrinking? To begin to answer it, I would suggest considering why, a few years ago, it was growing.

✧

30. More on Administration

This chapter developed in response to the following comment I received on my blog:

Dear Steve,

> *I came across your blog for the first time today and was impressed by [the] exchange on school governance.... I really responded to your words and was curious to know your specific thoughts on Administration, and what advice you would give to others on best practice.... You also talk about structure, and I wondered what was the lightest possible administrative structure you've encountered or could envisage?*

> Yours most warmly,
> *Nicola*

As I delve into this subject, I would like to start by noting that Rudolf Steiner never said that Waldorf schools should be "faculty run"; the phrase he used was "self-administered," by which I believe he meant "not administered by the state." At present this is already a reality much more for U.S. schools than for most European schools, for in the U.S. we have always enjoyed greater local control and freedom in how we educate our youth than have nations with more powerful ministries of education. That said, I've read that the U.S. Federal government provides roughly ten percent of educational funding in the U.S. and ninety percent of the (mostly unfunded) directives and mandates.

Given this, it's really tough to say that a good administrator in a Waldorf school should be somehow different, beyond her commitment to the mission of the school, from an administrator at another school. In my experience, the toughest part of the administrator's job is gaining the trust of the teachers. For this reason alone, it may be good for Waldorf schools to select an experienced teacher to hold this position. The problem is that it's a rare teacher who can be a good administrator. And if the administrator is seen by parents as being partial to teachers' points of view, trust erodes quickly.

On the other hand, the peculiar structure of Waldorf schools requires administrators to adapt to the school. By this, I refer primarily to the tension that often exists among parents, boards, and teachers' councils or colleges, especially when times are tough. Most Waldorf schools, by bylaw or practice, for example, simply don't give the power to hire and fire to one person. So an administrator, then, becomes a diplomat, a person with lots of responsibility but little authority, carrying messages from one camp to the other and attempting to negotiate a peaceful settlement.

When you ask about "lightest possible" or minimal structure, I think of the school at which I currently work. I'm a full-time teacher and the only administrator, and a part-time one at that. We have an office manager/assistant here three mornings a week, as well as an off-site, hourly book-keeper and a volunteer treasurer. Teachers pitch in to help with admissions events, open houses, and so on. Volunteer trustees handle fundraising, and our Core Faculty of about seven teachers meets weekly. Our Board meets monthly. We have as close to no administrative structure as it's possible to have, I believe.

By contrast, I know a school that was advised by a highly paid professional to hire a full-time fundraiser. The school did this and, three years in, has yet to raise close to the cost of the fundraiser's salary and benefits. And I don't believe this is a comment on the fundraiser's ability but, rather, on the school's inability to see that their situation, despite the recommendation of a consultant, simply doesn't warrant a full-time person devoted to development.

In creating structure, it's too easy, I believe, to copy what everyone else does—such as an admissions officer, a development person, a business manager, an administrator—even when the numbers don't justify it. This brings up another point, which is that of scale. Small schools can break even; large schools can break even. However, smallish schools that act like large schools will lose money. And no private school can afford to do that for long. And there is a "deadly middle ground." For many private schools, it occurs between roughly sixty students and 150 to 200 students. This middle ground is precisely where many Waldorf high schools find themselves, unfortunately.

In growing from a small school to a larger school, schools add administration as they grow, and are happy for the increase in students. When, a few years later, perhaps, enrollment declines, rather than facing the actuality of the situation, they often freeze salaries, cut salaries, add to workloads, or otherwise diminish the morale of the school.

This brings up another point: When schools act like their real business is to provide support for a community of like-minded adults, rather than to do all they can to educate the children in their care as well as possible, and, in the process, to spend the parents' tuition dollars as wisely and efficiently as possible, they quickly lose their way, creating a vicious spiral that leads to further loss of enrollment.

᭡

31. Beware "First Grade Readiness"

Many Waldorf schools leave it to kindergarten teachers to determine which children are "ready" for first grade. Parents are told, following assessment, whether or not, in the eyes of these teachers, their child is ready.

Often, assessments don't take place until late spring, leaving parents anxious and wondering what they will do if their child isn't "ready," and whether or not they will still have time to get him into another local private school's first grade? Parents may use the school's waffling as a time to look around. And sometimes they get excited—or see their children get excited—about the green grass on the other side of the fence.

You see, for parents, the issue is often *not* about whether the child is "first-grade ready," but whether or not the Waldorf school will promote him. A child judged not to be first grade ready, in my experience, is more likely to leave the school for first grade somewhere else—another Waldorf school or perhaps the local public school. It's relatively rare that parents are so committed to the school or to Waldorf education at all costs that they'll bow to the teachers' judgment in this case. I'm not saying the teachers are wrong; rather, I'm just saying that the language and process they use can unnecessarily alienate parents. A goal for a school could be to have any family that leaves—after being denied admission or after being counseled out for any reason—to wish fervently that they could have obtained the pearl they sought. Somehow, Harvard manages to do this and Waldorf schools don't.

And isn't such a process of determining first grade readiness like leaving high school admissions to the eighth-grade teacher? Or college admissions to high school teachers? Yes, teachers should take into account the recommendations of previous teachers, be it eighth grade or kindergarten, but determination should rest with the school or class or grade the child is entering, in almost every case. To that end, I think "first grade readiness" should more accurately and less politically, less ideologically, and more politely be called "elementary school admissions."

Most children are simply ready for first grade, anyway, based on "normal" development and birthday. Yet, often, a whole class of parents is held hostage to assessments made late in the kindergarten year. Wouldn't it make more sense to alert sooner the few parents of children for whom there's an issue—a true developmental delay, a real concern over birthdate—and let the others breathe easy? Shouldn't these parents know long before the spring of kindergarten of issues that they and their teachers may wish to address?

When children are assessed in the spring of their kindergarten year for admission to elementary school the following fall—half a year away—they still have almost ten per cent of a life to lead! So much can still change before then...

And this brings me to another point: Often there are children who apply directly to first grade after having attended a different, non-Waldorf, early childhood program. Are these children shipped to the Waldorf kindergarten to be assessed? No! They're interviewed by the first grade teacher or her proxy! Why the special treatment?

I understand that I'm writing about unusual circumstances. But, as a former school administrator, I know that it only takes one angry parent every other year or so to make a school's life really difficult. And don't forget that the early childhood program is the base on which the whole school is built. After all, if you have a small kindergarten, you can't expect a large first grade. And if you have a shrinking kindergarten, your operating budget for the foreseeable future is in jeopardy.

Also, the solution is so easy: changing the way we talk about things and not using the phrase "first grade ready"; talking directly to parents as partners in education; and acknowledging that, after all advice and recommendations, it's up to the elementary school to select the students it can teach.

⚘

32. How Many Waldorf Teachers Actually Teach the Same Elementary School Class for Eight Years?

About six years ago, one of my MSEd students, Ashwini Pawar, wrote her thesis on this question.

You cannot find Rudolf Steiner saying that teachers should work with the same class for so many years. He did say "several," yes. But precisely eight? No. And Mark Riccio has suggested that even Steiner's conception of elementary school was really only seven years, the eighth year being a requirement of Swiss school law.

So, Pawar examined ten years of class-teaching at six different Waldorf schools and discovered that only one in four teachers actually takes a class in a Waldorf school from first through eighth grade.

She also asked about what led to teachers leaving a class. Was it burnout, family changes such as moving or childbirth, termination? This is much harder to assess. Teachers don't necessarily leave for one reason alone. And teachers don't necessarily confess to burnout, or, especially, to being fired. Schools and administrators, too, on the advice of their lawyers, won't necessarily discuss employee termination. And, even if they would, teachers are often allowed or asked to resign before actually being fired. Regardless, as far as Pawar could tell, or at least as far as I can recollect, as I'm sorry to say I didn't keep a copy of her thesis, roughly half the reasons for teachers leaving a class job were positive—having a child, for instance—and roughly half were negative—burning out or being fired.

In this, Waldorf school teachers mirror all teachers. According to research done by Richard Ingersoll, nearly half of all teachers leave the profession within the first five years.[22] It's not a job for everyone, Waldorf or not.

What does this mean? Waldorf schools might do well to avoid presenting this ideal of "one teacher for eight years" as a reality. If parents are "sold" on the ideal, and, in the process, become unhealthily attached to a particular teacher, it can be a real blow to their affection for the school if a teacher leaves midstream. This assumes that schools continue to hold it as an ideal. To be fair, at least a few Waldorf schools now deliberately divide elementary faculties between lower elementary and middle school.

33. Have Better Faculty Meetings Now!

Here is the structure of Berkshire Waldorf High School weekly faculty meetings, which run sixty to ninety minutes and no longer. We begin around three o'clock and leave, in daylight, at no later than four-thirty, enough time for an hour at the gym and then dinner with the family.

Opening

2 minutes
We read from Rudolf Steiner's *Calendar of the Soul.*

Study

15–30 minutes
For the first part of our faculty meetings, we study an educational text by Rudolf Steiner. In the past few years, we've worked through *Education for Adolescents, Towards the Deepening of Waldorf Education,* and *Balance in Teaching,* and we're currently well into *Soul Economy.* We read a paragraph at a time, passing the text from person to person. When necessary, we stop to discuss or question, as long as necessary. Our progress is slow, but we are thorough. Teachers also bring in outside, that is, non-Steiner, non-anthroposophical, research when relevant. Sometimes we read one paragraph that provokes discussion for the rest of our time; sometimes we read several paragraphs without comment.

I would like to share one favorite story: In *Education for Adolescents,* Steiner makes a well-known and cryptic remark positing that the function of the human liver is analogous to the history of ancient Egypt. Rather than scratch our heads and read on, we decided to tackle this statement. To begin, our life science teacher characterized the function of the human liver. Then I, as a history teacher, gave a general overview of the history of ancient Egypt. By the end of this exercise, which took time in meetings over two weeks, it became clear that the concept of balance or homeostasis, and also the expulsion of toxins, related to both. The liver "cleans" the blood and maintains many physiological balances within each of us. And Egypt shows remarkable balance in politics and culture, including religion and artwork, through more than two thousand years of its history—and it repelled or expelled would-be invaders remarkably well.

Students

5–30 minutes

Teachers may request that any student be added to the agenda, but only for a positive, helpful purpose. In other words, you may not simply report that Giovanni isn't doing his homework; you must have a suggestion for how we can help Giovanni get his work in on time. And the suggestion has to be something that isn't simply to benefit your own classroom, but one that, if the whole faculty knows about it, will benefit Giovanni or the school as a whole.

Which of our students needs our attention? Is someone facing academic or emotional or social challenges? Is a clique forming? Are leaders leading? Do we have test results from a neuropsychological or psychoeducational exam? Are there behavior challenges that we need to address? Do we need to place a student on academic or behavioral probation? Are new students integrating well into the school? Is a student not completing work? Do we suspect abuse at home? Have we learned something that we find valuable to share among colleagues? Do we need to meet with a student or with his or her parents? Do we need to meet with a couple of students or with a small group of them?

I often say that half of our work is to teach the subjects we are hired to teach and the other half relates to the growth, maturation, health, and development of our students. Without appropriate, constructive attention, we may teach math brilliantly but fail to assist a student who is floundering in any number of other ways. During this portion of our meeting, teachers compare notes, achievements, results, and impressions in order to help every student in the school who needs help. We do not have a "child study" form or ritual, but we try to conduct this part of our meeting with an eye toward our most important work: teaching our students as well as we possibly can.

Calendar

1–10 minutes

Here we ask some questions: What is coming up in the next week or so that we all need to know about? Are there field trips, open houses, changes in the schedule, school events? Are we on the same page? Is everything planned that needs to be planned?

Business

15–45 minutes

Here we engage in a variety of subjects, including updating or clarifying policies and procedures; transportation planning (we're almost a school without walls each afternoon, and making sure everyone who needs a ride has a ride takes longer than it does at many other schools); discussing admission of new students (we have an Admissions Director, but, when each application is complete, it is brought to faculty meeting for a final decision on admission); reviewing reports on upcoming events and conferences; assessing recent events in order to improve them for the future, and; considering student proposals (we are not a democratic school, but we include student views and ideas as much as possible).

Closing

2 minutes
We read again from Rudolf Steiner's *Calendar of the Soul*.

Why Does This Work?

1. We give each item enough time for due consideration but no more. And each item may be considered only with a view to improving the school. We may criticize the way things are or have been done, but only if we have a reasonable, concrete, clear proposal for improvement. And if it becomes clear that we can't reach agreement in a reasonable time, the item is tabled for the next meeting.

2. We respect the school's history, ancient and modern. We're clear that in the absence of a decision to change, the default position, for better and worse, is the way things have been. Does one of us not like the way the opening assembly was conducted? Perhaps that person can suggest a change that we can all agree to, or it will continue as it has, whether the person likes it or not. The wheel does not need to be reinvented, but it benefits from evolutionary change.

3. Our agendas contain no last-minute entries. Did one of us forget to add something that we believe is important? We'll learn, and life will continue. As a group we learned from Caroline Estes, who represents Native American and Quaker streams of consensus decision-making, that "there are no emergencies." That said, when a rare real emergency does pop up, there's no time to decide if it's an emergency or not. For example: "The school is on fire; shall I put this item on the agenda? Or perhaps we should just go fight the fire?"

4. Although all faculty members are solicited for agenda items, the Faculty Chair creates the agenda, allots time, and decides—in conversation with faculty members outside the meeting—which items either don't belong on the agenda or may be addressed effectively outside the meeting.

5. We are clear that there are exactly two decision-making bodies in the school: the Board of Trustees, which has responsibility for the financial health and legal representation of the school, for planning, and for fundraising (we are remarkably conventional in this; that is, like other independent schools); and the Core Faculty. Administrators shepherd items but do not decide. And items that require Board and Faculty consideration are sent to a Board–Faculty Working Group (that can only send items to the Faculty or the Board for eventual decision). This ensures that there is no "meeting-after-the-meeting" at which decisions mysteriously change. Also, if one of us doesn't speak our mind in one of these two meetings, we simply have no other avenue to be effectively heard.

6. We work really hard to make decisions based on principle, not on particular circumstances or on personalities. And if a principle isn't clear, we back up to clarify it for ourselves before applying it.

7. Teachers and Board members serve on committees that may meet between Board or Faculty meetings, but, otherwise, we have no additional meetings in the week.

8. We're inclusive. Our admissions director, Board chair, business manager, part-time teachers, and even parent volunteers are invited to our meetings. Yes, there are occasions when we have to ask someone to step out for a brief executive session, but it's clear that these are times relating to possible conflicts of interest or confidentiality. We have a circle of teachers and others committed to the school, sometimes called a College of Teachers, but not an "inner circle."

9. We're a high school incorporated separately from our elementary school. Sometimes questions arise around this. Is someone concerned about differences in student dress guidelines between the two schools, for instance? Well, we have our own, and don't often have to worry about a conflict between our dress guidelines and theirs.

10. What? No group meditation? No. To our knowledge, Steiner never spoke of meditation as a group activity or as part of a faculty meeting.

Of course, our meetings are not perfect, nor is our school. We're human. Feelings get hurt. People are uncomfortable. People don't get their way. The schedule isn't ideal. The teaching isn't perfect. But, by focusing on our purpose as a school, we're pretty good at getting from week to week without profuse, lengthy, stressful, unproductive faculty meetings.

THE FUTURE

34. WHAT'S ESSENTIAL: FIVE GIFTS OF A STEINER SCHOOL EDUCATION

A Steiner school gives its graduates—its high school graduates, that is—five gifts. Primary school parents and graduates will recognize certain aspects of these gifts, but they will also recognize that they do not come to fruition by seventh or eighth grade.

1. A Steiner school provides the gift of ideas and ideals. However, a Steiner school does not provide beliefs or a worldview. Belief, knowledge, and worldview may be "about" spiritual matters, but are not them. The school provides a pathway or method for discovering profound ideas and ideals, should a student wish later in life to pursue them.

   In fact, all we can give with regard to spiritual realities—the realm of ideas and ideals—is a path that can be followed or retraced. In geometry, I can show you how certain steps lead to logical proof, but you must take that final intuitive leap yourself. If you do not "see" that these steps constitute a proof, all I can do as a teacher is retrace the path with you, perhaps using different language or different symbols in order to help you again to the brink of intuitive understanding.

2. A Steiner school addresses its students as developing human beings, beings uniquely capable of inner transformation. In nature, metamorphoses and transformations are primarily visible. We can see a plant grow

from shoot to leaves to flower, each stage presenting unforeseen changes of form. No one looking at a caterpillar for the first time would guess that it will soon become a butterfly. In human life, especially after childhood, transformation and development are not so visible. For Steiner, all cats belong to the same species, but each human being is a species unto himself or herself.

3. A Steiner school introduces students to different ways of knowing, three in particular. First, you can know cognitively. You can live in your head. You can contemplate or reflect, observe or compare, analyze or synthesize. This accords most closely with what the world outside a Steiner school means by "knowing."

   But you can also know with your heart. I call this aesthetic knowing, knowing in which you are awake to beauty, to an ethical understanding, and even to truth. The path to truth may be cognitive, but the recognition of truth is a feeling. Playfulness is the true expression of aesthetic knowing. One way to understand what I mean is to contrast aesthetic knowing with its opposite, "anaesthetic knowing." Something that anaesthetizes you puts you to sleep—you cannot know anything. The aesthetic awakens you.

   Last, you can know in your body and in your senses. Michael Polanyi calls this "tacit knowing," knowing more than we can say. You can read a book about playing the piano or performing heart surgery, but I hope you would not say after you put the book down that you knew how to do these things.

4. A Steiner school provides students profound examples and guidelines for a healthy life with other persons. If they choose to, Waldorf school graduates know how to care for others in brotherhood and sisterhood, in solidarity. They know how to respect the equality of any man or any woman. They know where their

individual freedom lies, the sort of freedom that laws and conventions cannot touch, and how to accord others their own freedom and dignity.

5. Finally, Steiner students receive a reverence for life and for the world, a concern for the environment, however defined. I mention this because as a society we have probably embraced this gift more fully in the past fifty years than we have the others.

Any school, any teachers, may give these gifts. But the sad truth is that in our world today only in Steiner schools can you regularly find teachers united in common purpose to give these gifts to their students as fully and consistently as possible.

✤

35. Chasing Insight Is Hard and Joyful Work

In a well-known story, Archimedes, when asked to determine whether or not a crown was made of gold or of a cheaper alloy, could not destroy the crown to assay it. So how could he determine whether the crown was pure or alloy? Imagine him puzzling over this apparently insoluble problem. Then, watching the way his body displaced water as he lowered himself into a bathtub, the answer struck him. He is said to have exclaimed, *"Eureka!"*—"I have found (it)."

He realized that if the crown and an equal weight of gold displaced equal amounts of water, then the crown was genuine. If the crown displaced more water than an equal weight of gold, then it was at least partly made of a less dense, and thus less valuable material—say, silver.

This story is supposed to demonstrate the lightning-like swiftness of insight[23] granted to geniuses like Archimedes, but, perhaps, not to you and me. Some research in creativity focuses on such "Aha!" moments. But there's a lot more to it than this, and the research of eminent scholars like the late Howard Gruber focuses on the context in which such moments of discovery occur.[24]

In that spirit, the following points are worth stating because, however obvious they may be, they are essential and instructive.

First, Archimedes stated the problem clearly for himself—or had it stated for him. Honing our questions so that we understand what we are asking and know that it really matter to us puts us on the path to insight.

Second, however brilliant Archimedes may have been, and he was probably among the more brilliant humans ever to live, he had a store of knowledge and experience, an education or self-education, perhaps acquired over years, at least about things like the differing densities of metals and about water in bathtubs. You simply can't have insights about matters of which you are ignorant. And, very often, insight comes in recognizing a solution to a problem in one area, like the purity of metals, with an insight from an apparently unrelated area—in this case, the displacing of water in a bathtub. A broad and deep education—not necessarily schooling, but education—provides the background from which insight may arise.

Third, Archimedes chose to live with the possibility that there was an answer to his problem and that he could discover it. Some problems have solutions that are only discovered years or even centuries after they are first posed. Other problems, perhaps, have no solutions. Regardless, if we do not approach problems with the understanding that they may be solved, we are unlikely to garner any insight.

Fourth, Archimedes spent time puzzling over this new problem, working on it—and we don't know for how long. I can picture him staring at the crown, hefting it in his hands. I picture him exhausting what he knew about such matters. How many days or weeks passed while the obdurate crown sat there, untested? Insight is generally granted to those who exert themselves, not to those who seek instant gratification.

Fifth, he let the problem go. At the least, he decided to take a bath. History is full of insights granted to those who take a walk, doodle in the sand, plow a field, lie back in a bedroom watching a fly, pick burrs off a dog, or simply take a bus or streetcar home.[25]

Sixth, Archimedes had an insight and recognized it as such. Chances are good that we each have several insights per day, although of a lower order than that of Archimedes, but neglect to recognize them, write them down, or pay attention to them.

Seventh, he recognized the truth of his solution even before he had worked out its details and put it to the test. It is common that a researcher will recognize a solution or a composer will "see" a symphony whole in his mind, even though it may take weeks, months, or even years to demonstrate the solution to a problem or complete the written score.

Meanwhile, it could easily have been the case, for example, that even though Archimedes knew he was correct, he was unable to prove it. Perhaps the difference in the amounts of water displaced might have been too small to measure using his antique equipment. In that case, he would have had to invent some new, more sensitive balance, conduct several trials, and think things through to eliminate error. But all of this thinking and work would still come after the moment of insight.

Eighth, we assume that he was willing to do the work necessary to prove that his insight was right, and not content simply to sit in a *taverna* and hold forth on his (untested) brilliance.

Ninth, he did the work, successfully. He could, after all, have been willing but unsuccessful, leaving it for later generations to prove him right.

Insight, then, is one moment within a larger context of inquiry and meaning. It is the pivot, we could say, between the work that leads up to it and the work that follows and tests it. All knowledge, in the end, is the result of insight; if not our own, then someone else's. When we were young and eager and curious and flexible, we gathered insights all the time and thought nothing of it, sort of like the way we stopped at nothing to learn to walk, despite failing for months and months, falling and falling. If we had to accomplish something so physically demanding today, would we do it? Or would we simply rationalize our lack of motivation as inability?

As we age, we tend to calcify, to ossify, to become less playful, less open to insight. But we needn't let this change overcome us. Although it's hard work to pursue insight, the path is clear, and it's a joyful one, too—so joyful that Archimedes, possessed by the joy of his insight, was said to have jumped out of his bath and run naked through the streets of Syracuse!

❧

36. THE FUTURE OF WALDORF EDUCATION

There are roughly fifty-three million K–12 schoolchildren in the United States.

Of this number, forty-four million (83 percent) attend public schools.

A few more than six million (11 percent) attend independent (private) schools.

Approximately 1.5 million (3 percent) are homeschooled, a number that has grown significantly in the past decade and continues to grow. Homeschooling, however, seems generally to be a reaction against available options—public or private—rather than a positive choice in itself. Can it represent a viable future for educating children in the United States? I don't believe so.

Meanwhile, about 1.1 million children (2 percent) attend charter schools, a number that is growing but, given the grassroots energy required and the opposition of school districts and teachers' unions, also seems unlikely to be a route to the solution of American educational ills.

Finally, lumping independent and public-charter Waldorf school students together yields a number around thirty thousand, or 1/18 of one percent (0.06 percent) of students in the U.S., and perhaps half a percent of private school students.

The number of independent Waldorf schools, which grew at a rate approximately doubling every ten years from the 1930s through the 1990s, appears to have plateaued. The curve is sigmoid; such a curve is sometimes called a saturation curve. That is, given the configurations of people's lives across roughly the past century, the demand for small, independent, relatively expensive, alternative Waldorf schools may be reaching its limit. Waldorf schools of this type may have saturated their possible markets.

It also seems like the failure rate for Waldorf schools—which was low through the first six decades in the U.S., is increasing. I don't have hard numbers here, but from what I have gathered only a handful of Waldorf schools closed. But it does seem like the conditions for the growth of new schools have changed. Maybe they're being founded in some new, less hardy way. Or maybe the greater cultural or economic climate has changed. Or maybe the way the schools themselves represent Waldorf education has become unpalatable. Regardless, it's certainly true that service industries like education can't benefit from economies of scale; hence the increasing cost of all education.

Now this is not to say that new private Waldorf schools won't continue to be founded, but that their survival will be less assured, their road to sustainability harder. But, without some fundamental change in how Waldorf schools see themselves and conduct themselves—or without some fundamental change in the conditions in which they exist—their growth will be arithmetic, or, let's say, not geometric.

If the path to the future includes growth, it is likely not private school growth. Perhaps it's public-school growth. There are between thirty and forty Waldorf charter schools (some call them "Waldorf-inspired," but I don't care for this distinction) in the U.S., and the number is likely to continue to grow as the charter movement grows. But for how long will this be true? What is the saturation of charter schooling in the U.S.? Urban districts can absorb charter schools, but rural districts cannot. Charter schooling seems not to be a panacea for public education in the U.S., and therefore not a permanent growth area for Waldorf schools.

Homeschooling, too, is burgeoning, and many home-schoolers receive an education that is based on Steiner's educational ideas. Yet how many homeschoolers use Waldorf methods, and how they interpret them, is impossible to say.

Altogether, however, charter schools and homeschoolers represent fewer than three million school-age children. We may estimate that, like private schools, they represent a higher percentage of Waldorf methods than public schools— say half a percent versus 1/20 of a percent, roughly an order of magnitude. If these numbers grow significantly, and if Waldorf methods grow as a constant percentage within this growth, they may represent the most significant possibility for the growth of the number of students receiving an education based on Steiner's ideas.

In the long run, however—the next decade or beyond—it seems unlikely that charter schools and homeschoolers offer real solutions to whatever ails American education. These movements exist within the framework of intractable teachers' unions, increasing education costs, and pressure toward standardization from Washington that seems not to change from administration to administration.

♦

37. Is Your School a Dinosaur? The Future of Education in the United States

Schools are headed toward extinction.

First, small private schools. Then larger private schools (except those few insulated by university-like endowments).

Then public schools—first the smaller districts, then the larger.

Why? Because as productivity, economies of scale, and automation effectively lower the prices of many goods, services that rely on human relationships become relatively and increasingly expensive. I believe this is called Baumol's Law, after the famous economist.

Education is headed the way of healthcare, following by a decade or two. Why is it following? Because, as costly as it is, education costs less than healthcare. Annually, we spend about $11,000 per person for healthcare; we spend about $12,000 per person for primary and secondary education, but only for the one-sixth of the population that is school age. Healthcare is about 18 percent of the GDP; education is between three and four percent.

Private schools can charge more, up to a point. Public schools can dun taxpayers, again, up to a point.

Eventually, we'll run out of wiggle room. Already, programs are cut, salaries are low, full-time positions are reduced, and buildings are going unmaintained. Homeschooling is up, but is a solution for only a privileged few. Charter schools, too, buffer some costs, but only by a bit; they are a band-aid, not a cure.

Growing income inequality and wealth disparity only make these circumstances worse.

Schools will close and go out of business. That's the bad news.

Is there any good news?

Yes.

First, students still need to be educated, regardless of the economy that blankets their parents' lives. And if our educational models aren't working, we'll need to turn to others.[26]

Larger, centralized school districts may seem to be the answer, but transportation costs and travel times make this model harder, not easier. For example, a school bus currently costs more than $1,000 per year per student. More important, large campuses with facilities and rooms that are used for a fraction of a day for a fraction of a year, such as swimming pools and athletic fields, theaters, and classrooms, are not efficient to construct or maintain. Given factory-like Taylorism (efficiency), professionalization of teaching and administration, and the wealth created after World War II, we created schools that now look a lot like dinosaurs—large, slow, and not too smart.

Schools will be driven to become smaller, more flexible, more creative, and more integrated into their communities. Perhaps they will use a school library or town library. Perhaps they will use a town pool with hours reserved for the school's swim team. Perhaps they will have classrooms that can be used as community rooms after hours. Shared facilities and shared costs will make these things possible. Flexible, creative, smaller community schools can be more cost effective, especially because the Internet does allow many functions, including much administration and business administration, to be centralized and consolidated even when students aren't.

Meanwhile, don't forget that American schools are as much about sports as they are about education. Can there be football at a small school? Yes, with work. Little League and Cal Ripkin baseball have existed for decades without school involvement.

These smaller, more flexible schools of the near future are like the small mammals that supplanted the dinosaurs. They're coming. Are you ready?

ENDNOTES

1   I do not mean too broadly to categorize Waldorf schools or teachers, or other teachers or schools. There are great teachers in many, even most schools, teachers who are well aware of and foster their students' curiosity, intellectual, and personal development in brilliant and creative ways.

2   Please allow me to share two quotations from Steiner:

> Above all, we must try to cultivate as much simple speaking and conversation with the children as possible during the first year. We read aloud as little as possible, but instead prepare ourselves so well that we can bring to them in a narrative way whatever we want to tell them. Then we seek to reach the point where the children are able to retell what they have heard from us. We avoid using passages that do not stimulate the imagination and make as much use as possible of texts that activate the imagination strongly, namely, fairy tales—as many fairy tales as possible. Having practiced this telling and retelling with the children for a long time, we start in a small way to let them give brief accounts of experiences they themselves have had. We let the children relate something they like talking about. With all this telling and retelling of stories and personal experiences, we develop the transition from the local vernacular to educated speech by simply correcting mistakes the children make, without being pedantic about it. At first they will make many mistakes, but later fewer and fewer. Through telling and retelling, we develop in the children the transition from vernacular to educated speech. In this way, the children will have reached the desired goal by the end of their first year at school. (Rudolf Steiner, *Practical Advice to Teachers*, pp. 168–169)

> When the children arrive at school on the following morning they have, without knowing it, pictures of the previous day's experiments in their heads, as well as pictures of what—in as imaginative a way as possible—I repeated, recapitulated after the experiment. The children I then confront have photographs of the previous day's experiment in their heads. And I shall now reflect on yesterday's lesson in a contemplative way. Yesterday I experimented, and in reviewing the experiment I then appealed to the children's imagination. In today's lesson I add the contemplative element. In doing so, I

not only meet the pictures in the children's heads, but also help to bring the pictures into their consciousness. (Rudolf Steiner, *Education for Adolescents*, pp. 51–53)

[Note: Because this final quotation—and several other that will follow—come from Steiner's *Education for Adolescents*, which is not widely read, it is not well-enough known among Waldorf school teachers. The lectures in this collection were given as a course, following *Balance in Teaching*, to all teachers at the first Waldorf school, and address far more than simply the education of adolescents. The title is a misnomer, and the book deserves to be read and reread by all teachers who want to know more about Steiner's method. Each successive course that Steiner offered occurred after he'd had more time to see his ideas applied in classrooms, and therefore contains an accumulation of wisdom and insight that we cannot afford to ignore.]

3   "In the first part, I occupied their whole being; in the second, it is the rhythmic part of their being that must make an effort. I then dismiss them" (Rudolf Steiner, *Education for Adolescents*, pp. 51–53).

4   "Never underestimate the effect of the unknown or half known. The effect of such on feeling is extremely important. If toward the end of a lesson we say, 'and tomorrow we shall do this...'—the children need not know anything about 'this'; their expectation and curiosity will still be aroused. If, for example, I have taught the properties of the square before those of the triangle and I conclude the lesson by saying, 'Tomorrow we shall learn about the triangle'—the children do not yet know anything about the triangle, but it is exactly this fact that causes a certain tension, an expectation of what is to come, a looking forward to the next day's lesson. The effect will carry the day. We ought to make use of the unknown or half known in order to facilitate the children's effort at fitting the details into a totality. We really must not ignore such matters" (Rudolf Steiner, *Education for Adolescents*, pp. 19–20).

5   "The children will present to you on the following morning the results of what they experience between falling asleep and waking" (Steiner, *Education for Adolescents*, p. 47).

"If we ignore the fact that the content of our lessons continues into sleep, develops further during sleep, we will have the quite definite effect of making the human being into a robot, an automaton" (Rudolf Steiner, *Education for Adolescents*, p. 58).

6   My intention is not to make anyone feel bad. Yet perhaps you just did what this chapter calls into question and then, on your coffee break, you read this chapter. Don't feel bad. Just use this as a spur to research, and, if necessary, do better! We can

all always improve. And I mean all, including me. Kids are resilient. And breaking with dogma or convention doesn't mean doing whatever you like, but replacing an older, less thought-imbued practice with a new, experimental, conscious, thoughtful practice. Also, we are all free (probably), and you may choose to ignore whatever I write or to form your own opinion of the matter. Be safe out there.

7   Wiley-Blackwell. "Do Doodle: Doodling Can Help Memory Recall." ScienceDaily. ScienceDaily, Mar. 5, 2009. [https://www .sciencedaily.com/releases/2009/02/090226210039.htm]

8   Meier, A. (2016). "Oklahoma City School Discovers More 1917 Chalkboards Hidden in Its Walls"; retrieved online from: https: //hyperallergic.com/268571/oklahoma-city-school-discovers-more -1917-chalkboards-hidden-in-its-walls/

9   I'm indebted to Christine Cox Good, a former student at Sunbridge College, for tracking the math gnomes to their source in her unpublished 2006 MSEd thesis, "In Search of Math Gnomes."

10   Here's a note on my method, for those wishing to compile other such collections of Steiner quotations on various topics, especially on education. Almost all of Steiner's educational lectures and publications are available as free downloads, usually as PDFs, from the SteinerBooks spiritual research archive. Once you have downloaded these, it becomes a simple and enlightening matter, if somewhat time consuming, to search on key terms (e.g., *arithmetic, math*), then read, copy, and paste.

11   This way of describing the soul puts me in mind of the German-American psychologist Kurt Lewin, specifically his research into gestalt psychology and his theory of psychological "force fields."

12   I write "According to Steiner," but it's also self-evident for reflective persons that what we call feelings or emotions mediate our thinking and our willing. For more on this, I would recommend studying Jürgen Habermas's concept of a "Lifeworld," in his book *The Theory of Communicative Action*, vol. 2.

13   Germans have several other words for body: *Leib*, or body, in a more poetic sense; *Körper*, or body, in a more scientific sense and also in the sense of a whole, a corpus; and *Leiche*, or corpse. Steiner uses these terms, too, when appropriate. With the exception of the word *corpse*, it is challenging for translators to capture the words' nuances and connotations. Also, to avoid the challenge I've outlined above, translators sometimes use the word *sheath* to suggest the matryoshka-doll-like image that Steiner's descriptions of human existence produce. However, I find this usage somewhat misleading, somewhat archaic, and also somewhat peculiar.

14   I am indebted to Jean-Michel David of Melbourne, Australia for some of the research into uses of the word *anthroposophy* before Steiner.

15   For more on this topic, see: (1) Sagarin, S. (2007). "Playing 'Steiner Says:' Twenty Myths about Waldorf Education." In *Research Bulletin*, vol. 12, no. 2, spring 2007, pp. 37–44. Wilton, NH: Research Institute for Waldorf Education. (2) Howard, S. (2006). "The Essentials of Waldorf Early Childhood Education." In *Gateways*, 51, fall/winter, pp. 6–12. Spring Valley, NY: WECAN [http://www.waldorfearlychildhood.org/uploads /Howard%20Article.pdf], and (3) Wiechert, C. (2011). "Rethinking the Threefold Division of the Main Lesson." [http: //www.waldorftoday.com/2011/01/rethinking-the-threefold -division-of-the-main-lesson-christof-weichert/]

16   Steiner, in *Faculty Meetings with Rudolf Steiner*, vol. 2, p. 558: "The use of the French language quite certainly corrupts the soul. The soul acquires nothing more than the possibility of clichés. Those who enthusiastically speak French transfer that to other languages. The French are also ruining what maintains their dead language, namely, their blood."

17   NPR: "Preschool: The Best Job-Training Program," Aug. 12, 2011. Retrieved online: https://www.npr.org/sections/money /2011/08/12/139583385/preschool-the-best-job-training-program

18   I am indebted to my students at Sunbridge Institute for helping me clarify several aspects of this chapter; it attempts to summarize a week of work in an intensive course on school governance.

19   I use the phrase "rights and responsibilities," because I believe that to be more revealing in this context than the word *politics,* which is tainted in contemporary colloquial use, and more revealing than *legal,* which doesn't go far enough to describe what I'm talking about. And I include *responsibilities,* because these are clearly conceptually necessary, with *rights,* to describe what I'm talking about. Steiner includes them, although this is often overlooked or forgotten. To call it a "rights" administration alone indulges a kind of knee-jerk American selfishness—"I insist on my rights"—and ignores the obligations that we owe each other in social interactions.

20   This chapter is prompted by years of work in Waldorf schools, by recent conversations about the current travails of a particular school that is struggling with shrinking enrollment, and by a recent glance through the financial statements of half a dozen Waldorf schools.

21   For the record, I have now been a teacher-administrator for the past thirteen years.

22   *Penn Graduate School of Education News* (Oct. 23, 2018). "The Teacher Workforce Is Transforming: Here's What It Means for Schools and Students"; retrieved online: https://www.gse.upenn.edu/news/teacher-workforce

23   For the purposes of this chapter 1, have chosen to use the word *insight*, though I could just as easily refer to it as "imagination" or "inspiration."

24   One of Gruber's books is appropriately titled *Creative People at Work.*

25   Of note, here is a list of those who are known to have received insight while doing the activities listed above: Beethoven (taking a walk), Norman Woodland, the inventor of the barcode (doodling in the sand), Philo Farnsworth, inventor of the television (plowing a field), Rene Descartes, the developer of the Cartesian plane (lying back in a bedroom watching a fly), George de Mestral, the inventor of Velcro (picking burrs off a dog), August Kekule, the founder of the theory of chemical structures (taking a bus home), and Einstein, who demonstrated mass-energy equivalence (taking a streetcar home).

26   Perhaps some will begin arguing for online education. I believe there's some utility here, but not much. Research increasingly shows that learning from screens is suboptimal in many ways. And we can't expect, nor should we want, a computer to replace a human being as a teacher.

References

Arbesman, S. *The Half-Life of Facts*. New York: Penguin, 2012.

Aristotle. *Nicomachean Ethics*, Book 2, 3rd ed. Indianapolis: Hackett Publishing, 2019.

Barfield, O. *History, Guilt and Habit*. UK: Barfield Press, 2012.

———. *Romanticism Comes of Age*. Letchworth, Hertfordshire, UK: Rudolf Steiner Press, 1966.

———. *Speaker's Meaning*. Middletown: Wesleyan University, 1967.

Bortoft, H. *The Wholeness of Nature: Goethe's Way toward a Science of Conscious Participation in Nature*. Great Barrington, MA: Lindisfarne Books, 1996.

Campbell, J. and D. Osbon. *Reflections on the Art of Living*. New York: HarperPerennial, 1991.

Cox, C. "In Search of Math Gnomes: First Grade Arithmetic in Waldorf Schools." Unpublished MSEd thesis. Sunbridge College, New York, 2006.

Freedman, R. *Martha Graham: A Dancer's Life*. New York: Clarion Books, 1998.

Goethe, J. W. von. "The Metamorphosis of Plants." In D. Miller (ed. and tr.), *Goethe's Scientific Studies*. Princeton, NJ: Princeton University, 1988.

———. *Theory of Colors*. Cambridge, MA: The M.I.T, 1970.

Habermas, J. *Theory of Communicative Action*, vol. 2. Boston: Beacon Press, 1985.

Harrer, D. *Math Lessons for Elementary Grades*. Longmont, CO: AWSNA, 2013.

Heydebrand, C. von. *Curriculum of the First Waldorf School*. Longmont, CO: Aelzina Books 2021.

Hocks, E. "Dialectic And The 'Two Forces Of One Power': Reading Coleridge, Polanyi, and Bakhtin in a New Key," *Tradition and Discovery: The Polanyi Society Periodical*, vol. 23, no. 3, 1996: pp. 4–16.

Lewis, C. S. "Men Without Chests." In *The Abolition of Man*. San Francisco: HarperOne, 2001.

Niederhauser, H., et al. *Towards the Deepening of Waldorf Education*. Dornach: The Pedagogical Section of the School of Spiritual Science, 2006.

Plato. *Laches and Charmides*. Indianapolis: Hackett, 1992.

Riccio, M.-D. *An Outline for a Renewal of Waldorf Education: Rudolf Steiner's Method of Heart-thinking and its Central Role in the Waldorf School*. Spring Valley, NY: Mercury Press, 2002.

Schuberth, E. *Mathematic Lessons for the Sixth Grade*. Chatham, NY: Waldorf Publications, 2002.

———. *Teaching Mathematics for First and Second Grades in Waldorf Schools*. Fair Oaks, CA: Rudolf Steiner College, 1999.

Sloan, D. "Declaration of Douglas Sloan in Support of Defendants' Opposition to Plaintiff's Motion for Summary Judgment..." Case no. 104. S-98-0266 FCD PAN. PLANS, Inc. v. Sacramento City Unified School District, Twin Ridges Elementary School District, DOES 1–100. United States District Court, Eastern District of California. July 30, 2004.

St. Charles, D. Interview by Alan Chartock on WAMC, 90.3 FM, Northeast Public Radio, Albany, NY. April; 1994 (exact date unavailable). Reference obtained from undated cassette tape recording.

Steiner, R. *Balance in Teaching*. New York: Mercury Press, 1982.

———. *The Calendar of the Soul: Facsimile Edition*. Great Barrington, MA: SteinerBooks, 2003.

———. *The Child's Changing Consciousness*. Hudson, NY: Anthroposophic Press, 1996.

———. *Discussion with Teachers*. Hudson, NY: Anthroposophic Press, 1997.

———. *Education as a Force for Social Change*. Hudson, NY: Anthroposophic Press, 1997.

———. *Education for Adolescents*. Hudson, NY: Anthroposophic Press, 1996.

———. *Faculty Meetings with Rudolf Steiner*, 2 vols. Hudson, NY: Anthroposophic Press, 1998.

————. *Foundations of Human Experience*. Hudson, NY: Anthroposophic Press, 1996.

————. *Kingdom of Childhood*, rev. ed. Hudson, NY: Anthroposophic Press, 1995.

————. *Mission of Folk-Souls*, 2nd ed. Forest Row, UK: Rudolf Steiner Press, 1970.

————. *The Philosophy of Freedom*. Forest Row, UK: Rudolf Steiner Press, 2011.

————. *Practical Advice to Teachers*. Hudson, NY: Anthroposophic Press, 2000.

————. *Renewal of Education*, 2nd ed. Hudson, NY: Anthroposophic Press, 2002.

————. *Soul Economy*, rev. ed. Hudson, NY: Anthroposophic Press, 2003.

————. *The Spiritual Ground of Education*. Hudson, NY: Anthroposophic Press, 2000.

————. *Theosophy*. Hudson, NY: Anthroposophic Press, 1994.

————. "The Threefold Social Order and Educational Freedom." In *The Renewal of the Social Organism*. Hudson, NY: Anthroposophic Press, 1996.

————. *Towards the Deepening of Waldorf Education*. Dornach: The Pedagogical Section Council, 1991.

————. *Towards Social Renewal*, 3rd ed. Forest Row, UK: Rudolf Steiner Press, 1992.

Stockmeyer, E. *Rudolf Steiner's Curriculum for Steiner-Waldorf Schools: An Attempt to Summarise His Indications*. Stourbridge, UK: Floris Books, 2015.

Vowell, S. *The Wordy Shipmates*. New York: Riverhead Books, 2009.

Whitehead, A. *The Aims of Education and Other Essays*. New York: Free Press, 1929/1967.

Whitman, W. *Leaves of Grass*. New York: HarperCollins, 1986.

Yeats, W. B. *The Collected Poems of W. B. Yeats*. Hertfordshire, England: Wordsworth Editions, 1994.

Also by Stephen Keith Sagarin

THE STORY OF WALDORF EDUCATION IN THE UNITED STATES
Past, Present, and Future

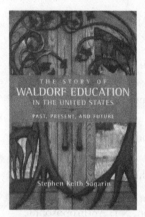

Representing more than a decade of research, this book is the first account of the history and development of Waldorf education in America. Looking at the past and present with an eye to how the understanding of the term *Waldorf education* has changed over time, the author identifies key trends in education, both Waldorf and general education, to imagine the direction in which Waldorf education may move in the future.

The book shows how the number of Waldorf schools grew slowly and steadily and how they have evolved through four generations, examining the methods and myths of Waldorf education and showing what is essential and what is extraneous. The author reveals Waldorf education as what many believe Rudolf Steiner, its founder, intended it to be: a living method of education that may be employed by any teacher or any school.

The author concludes that Waldorf education is not a method that can be packaged and sold, but a living method that depends on insight for continual renewal.

ISBN 9780880106566 | pbk | 220 pgs

About the Author

Stephen Keith Sagarin, PhD, is faculty chair, a cofounder, and a teacher at the Great Barrington Waldorf High School in western Massachusetts, where he teaches history and life science. He is also a former teacher and administrator at the Great Barrington Rudolf Steiner School and the Waldorf School of Garden City, New York, the high school from which he graduated. Dr. Sagarin writes, lectures, mentors teachers, and consults with Waldorf schools on teaching and administration. He is an associate professor and director of the MS education program in Waldorf teacher education at Sunbridge Institute, New York. He is the former editor of the *Research Bulletin of the Research Institute for Waldorf Education* and has taught history of education at Teachers College, Columbia University, New York City; human development at the City University of New York; and U.S. and world history at Berkshire Community College, Massachusetts. Dr. Sagarin has a PhD in history from the Graduate School of Arts and Sciences, Columbia University, and a bachelor's degree in art history, with a certificate of proficiency in fine art, from Princeton University. He is married and the father of two children, Andrew and Kathleen. His wife, Janis Martinson, is Chief Advancement Officer at Miss Hall's School in Pittsfield, Massachusetts.